Teaching Dramatically
Learning Thematically

by
Laura Gardner Salazar

NEW PLAYS INCORPORATED
P.O. Box 5074
Charlottesville, VA 22905

DEDICATION

to Hugo, Tony and Kate

PREFACE

I well remember the excitement, many years ago, of sitting in a hotel ballroom at a conference of children's theatre and child drama teachers, and watching Dorothy Heathcote do her first big demonstration in America of "teaching in role." There was a large crowd of us, for her fame had preceded her, and there was a hush when she gathered up a group of 9 and 10 year olds and proceeded to create a drama with them before our eyes.

What she was doing stood "traditional" creative drama on its ears. There she was in the middle of the group, not directing, not playwriting, not side-coaching, but planting herself in the arena, larger than life, playing a part, sometimes a bit part and sometimes a lead, working right alongside the children in developing a dramatic idea. And sometimes she stopped the drama to talk about it, right in the middle!

What she was doing was breaking down the traditional hierarchy of teacher and student, blurring the traditional lines between acting and discussing. It was our introduction to "teaching in role," and I think it's fair to say that drama teaching in America has never since been quite the same. Right away the cult began to grow. The "Dorothy Heathcote method" was the new buzz-word. Move over, Viola Spolin. Move over, Brian Way. We had a new messiah.

Drama leaders began to adopt the mystique of "passwords" — terms Heathcote had used. It became fashionable to give children the "mantle of the expert," Heathcote's phrase for putting children in roles where they had authority and inside information. "Brotherhoods" were hot. Dorothy Heathcote stories passed for currency at theatre conferences. There grew up an inner circle of disciples who had sat at the feet of the master, not just at the seminars and courses she held at Northwestern University and elsewhere in the United States, but actually abroad, at her home base in England.

Others, meanwhile, said that nobody but Dorothy Heathcote could "do" Dorothy Heathcote, and we were being fools to try.

Since she could never be pinned down to write a book, someone else did it for her — Betty Jean Wagner in *Drama as a Learning Medium*, an excellent summation of Dorothy Heathcote at work. Liz Johnson and Cecily O'Neill gathered up her wisdom in *Dorothy Heathcote: Collected Writing on Education and Drama*. Meanwhile the waiting list grew longer to check out "Three Looms Waiting," a film showing Heathcote at work.

Today the "movement" does not seem quite so fanatic, but it is still alive and well. There are Dorothy Heathcote seminars and conferences in this country and abroad that attract students and teachers from all over the world.

Meanwhile that great lady, now semi-retired, goes blithely on doing what she does best, rarely committing a word to print, thus leaving herself free to evolve her ideas and change her mind when her work takes her in new directions.

I think of Dorothy Heathcote in that tradition of great British educators — Peter Slade and Brian Way come to mind in the field of child drama - whose theories and practices have made a solid impact on our work. And we, in turn, when the fever of hero worship has died down, have taken their ideas and made them our own, "naturalizing" them to American soil, adapting them to our own climatic conditions, strengthening them by cross-fertilization with our own best work.

Nobody has done this better than Laura Gardner Salazar in the book you now have in your hands. Taking her inspiration from Dorothy Heathcote's "thematic drama," she has developed a coherent, well-organized approach to using drama as a teaching tool in American schools. Her pages have their share of quotes and examples from the work of Dorothy Heathcote and Cecily O'Neill, the British educator who has continued demonstrating and popularizing the techniques of teaching in role. But she draws, as well, upon new currents of thinking about thematic teaching, communication theory, and the research that is giving us new understanding about multiple intelligences. Her education in classic theatre, and her 30 years of practice, in professional and educational settings, in interpreting and directing plays, help shape her thinking.

But above all, these pages are the work of the writer herself, who shares herself, her values, her years of experience teaching thematically in a university setting and also with children in classrooms, museums, church basements and unused TV studios. Her detailed accounts of thematic lessons include disappointments as well as triumphs. Through theory and example, she invites beginning drama leaders — and those still young enough at heart to make new beginnings — to join in a new style of thematic teaching and learning.

Patricia Whitton
Charlottesville, Virginia
November, 1994

INTRODUCTION

Early in the 1970's, I began experimenting with leading drama in role. I had just seen Dorothy Heathcote demonstrate her work in Chicago and Adrian, Michigan. I was fascinated. Working in role appeared to throw the players into much deeper concentration and thought than the creative drama styles dominating the American scene at that time. And it looked like so much fun! Over the years I continued to work in this style — at my studio, in summer camps, and always with my own university students in our work with groups of local children, adapting the style to the American scene.

By the time my sabbatical in 1985 took me to Dorothy Heathcote on her own territory, I had many thematic dramas under my belt. Meetings, discussion and video tapes at the University of Newcastle Upon Tyne broadened my scope. When I came home I began to work in earnest with more groups of children. I set out to devise a way to teach this style of drama to American teachers with the goal in mind to teach a world view, not merely a technique. I wanted to show how teaching theatre and teaching through theatre provide a natural and exciting way of exploring joys and solving problems.

When, in the early 1990's, I heard about the thematic teaching movement, I wondered why the in-role style of drama, with its emphasis on large themes that were suited so well to sweep across the curriculum, had not been pressed into service by those in the thematic movement.

In 1994 we find ourselves in a nation where standards in art education have become the law of the land and an important part of education reform. The focus in the Theatre Standards document falls on the study of the theatre as an art form. Because thematic drama lessons are based on the classic elements and structures of theatre, they fit well within the guidelines of these new National Standards. This book seeks to help drama leaders combine a holistic view, artistic techniques and the new curriculum reform.

Because thematic drama is difficult to talk about in theory without showing it in practice, I have made frequent reference to the sample lessons in Part Two, particularly "The Potawatomis of Pearline," which is described in some detail. Readers may want to look at this and other lessons as they go along.

I encourage my readers to carry the work forward, constructing theatre for young people in the mode of the playwright, presenting it in the mode of the actor, and using the world as a tool and playground for learning, all with honor to Dorothy Heathcote.

Laura Gardner Salazar
Grand Rapids, Michigan
November, 1994

CONTENTS

USING THE THEMATIC APPROACH

*"Drama honors the whole person, so we
don't have to leave anything at home."*
Dorothy Heathcote

This chapter introduces

• *the thematic style of drama;*

• *the place of drama in the curriculum;*

• *and the characteristics of a good drama leader.*

IT IS THE STATE'S SESQUECENTENNIAL. The work that is to be done has
to have truth and beauty, excitement and historical significance. The players,
twelve boys and girls aged eight through ten, and two leaders, Tammy
Holmden and myself, gather in a circle. I address the group:

> "I am going to walk away, and when I return I will be a character
> in our play. I will ask you some questions and I want you to
> answer them as if you were in the play, too. Wait and see, and you
> will discover who I am, who Tammy is, and even who you are.
> (*Pause*).

> "Oh, I am so glad to see you. My husband, Mr. Allen, said you
> might be here. He's gone to Muskegon to get supplies. And
> (*afraid and hesitant*) . . . do you understand me? He said the
> Indians would be able to help. Is Princess Sunflower here?"

> "Yes," answers Tammy. "I am Princess Sunflower. What can I do
> for you?"

> "I heard this sniffing sound outside my cabin all night. I think it
> was a wolf. It made me afraid. Do I need to be afraid of wolves?"

And thus began a ten-hour thematic drama entitled, "The Potawatomis of
Pearline," set in the daily life, arts and political reality of Michigan 150 years.
A complete description of the way the drama progressed, and a discussion of
the work, is presented on page 89. That lesson is an example of informal drama
in the thematic style, where one large sweeping theme is used to take players
into themselves and the world, investigating human relationships. It plunges
the players into imagined circumstances where they grapple with life-affecting
decisions. It emphasizes how all people in all times share certain moral, ethical and physical dilemmas whose resolution affects the future, perhaps for
many generations. Play centers around understanding consequences and solving problems.

The goal of the leader is to move the group to deep feelings and thoughts
within an artistic framework. By casting themes and enigmas into dramatic
metaphors, using dramatic circumstance, character and atmosphere, leaders are
able to tap players' ordinarily inaccessible senses of awe and wisdom. The

1

work is realized with both leaders and players alternating between playing roles and planning an aesthetic experience.

In thematic drama the leader himself often becomes one of the participants in the dramatic exploration of plot and character. By working alongside the players, the leader encourages belief, builds life-like situations, and helps players assume new sensitivities and responsibilities. The leader encourages the group to create partnerships as they explore problems and develop solutions.

Thematic drama adds the consideration of character and ethics to problem-solving. Dorothy Heathcote, the Englishwoman who pioneered thematic drama in role, says of the form, "You must teach who you are." Drama provides safe, visceral experiences. A large part of theatre's aesthetic power lies in a sense of relationship between the player and the role he assumes. Heathcote calls this heightened empathy the "brotherhoods." When a child takes on the role of a king, for example, he becomes part of the brotherhood of all those who have great power and must exercise great responsibility. Through exercising imagination, players come to realize they belong to many brotherhoods, facing the same basic needs, the same moral questions, the same relationships of love and hate for others as all humans throughout history and around the globe.

How thematic drama meets educational goals

Thematic drama supports new findings on how the brain works. Howard Gardner's revolutionary work at Harvard on the multiple intelligences is a case in point. Gardner points to the individual's use of several intelligences to solve problems. He also notes that drama parallels life, using all of the intelligences in its practice. Since the drama is reflective of the life experience, the thinking it models is accessible and useful to all.

Thematic dramas give experience in leadership, adaptability and flexibility. They provide a laboratory for hypothesizing. Thinkers make "educated guesses" as adults, much as they did in their dramatic play as young children. Thematic drama also encourages creative thinking. It is characterized by discovery, assessment and action.

When a class of eight and nine year olds chose to explore themes from the book *Only One Woof* by James Herriot, players used leadership skills when they solved a problem of sickness in the dogs. They used adaptability and flexibility by developing a situation in the book, creating dog trials in which the hero would give his only woof. They experienced flexibility as they agreed to accept each other's ideas. They hypothesized as they planned to raise money for prizes at the trials. They used creative thinking in suggesting prizes such as a jumping bar in the shape of a bone.

Theatre brings form and purpose to thought and emotion. To put this in metaphorical terms, drama provides the vessel for the event, and the players fill that vessel. Each historical age seems to provide a particular thought that characterizes its theatre. For the Greeks, drama's great concern was what constituted justice. For the Elizabethans, the concern of dramatic literature was what made a good and just monarch. For the realistic playwrights of this century, individual development and fulfillment were the central concerns. For the blacks in the townships of South Africa in modern times, drama centered on equality and justice. In every case, the drama has provided a forum for these concerns.

As with a playwright, it is the task of the drama leader to discover ways to fill the form with substance. This can come from the curriculum which is already in place, and can fit both old and new frameworks for teachers.

Thematic drama can be used successfully with today's pedagogy and curriculum. It provides new ways of arranging established ideas. The drama may take any subject of the curriculum for its thought, augmenting and assessing the curriculum already in place. It enhances the curriculum by adding new subject matter without disrupting daily and weekly time schedules. It reaches the learner where he is. It demands the same skills of teachers that it demands of students.

How thematic drama ties in with Integrated Thematic Instruction

School systems across the country are adopting Integrated Thematic Instruction. One of its chief proponents, Susan Kovalik, author of ITI: The Model (Oak Creek, AZ: Books for Educators, 1993) ties the new brain research to the thematic method of teaching. She writes,

> . . . *meaningfulness for elementary students must begin with first-hand, **being there**, here and now experiences. They provide the mental scaffolding for the words which represent the concepts and definitions of things they have experienced.* (p. 43)

She goes on to say that the neat, orderly, closely planned methods used by most teachers do not reflect the way people learn. Learning needs to reflect the chaos and interconnectedness of opportunities to choose. Thematic drama provides a means for bringing ITI'a "here and now" experiences into the classroom, empowering young people as they cannot be empowered elsewhere.

Much of our life is structured by others. In school children must follow the adult agenda, often eroding their motivation. In thematic drama, on the other hand, young people's own interests and questions can be perused seriously at a reasonable pace. In addition to empowerment, this style also demands that young people have the opportunity to try out what it is like to live with their mistakes.

Susan Kovalik describes a lesson designed to last one month with first and second graders on the subject of spiders. The study divided into the areas of "Life Cycle," "Cooperative Spiders," "Habitat," "Relationship to Man,"

"Caring," Collecting," and Feeding." The lessons used multi-aged and cooperative learning groups in the research which led to becoming experts. The children viewed themselves in the role of scientists. The analysis of the lesson (pp. 289-290) indicates that the teachers of the lesson wished to have improved "our learning celebration," and "the connectedness of concepts." Teachers also wished to move to a level where the students could make their own inquiries.

A deeper involvement with the arts, and theatre in particular, would have improved all three: celebration, connectedness and inquiry. As it was taught, the only "theatre" in the lesson was something called "spider charades." From the drama point of view, what seems to be lacking in the "spider charades" is motivation, emotion, values and relationships.

Drama provides a why for learning. What will knowing about spiders do for me? For my family and friends? What has it done for others in the past? Why did the first scientists study spiders? How do native peoples relate to to spiders in the natural world? How has the fear of spiders affected human beings? What happens when a dangerous spider is on the loose? All of Kovalik's topics could have been covered in thematic drama: "We need to keep species of spiders thriving;" "We need to know which spiders cooperate with us;" "In what places can we find spiders?" "How can we care for them?" "How can they be collected?" "What should we feed them?" Because the emphasis in this unit was on the world of real spiders, a dramatization of some of the many wonderful stories where spiders talk and do fantastical things — *Charlotte's Web* and the African Anansi stories come to mind — could appear late in the month's theme and provide celebration.

A way to achieve connectedness and self inquiry might be to throw the young players into a world where their beloved pets needed surgery. Only the natural anesthetic of the spider's poison would be able to save them. Players could study many species to find the best poison. They could learn how to extract the matter from the spider. They could learn to control the amount and how to work under dangerous conditions. They could work with the possibility of a poisonous spider getting loose. They could search for antidotes for a poisonous bite. The time and place of the drama could be in the present or the past or with a specific group of ethnic peoples who have used something from the spider to make their life better. Although the leader of the drama would set up the initial dramatic incident, the children would contribute to the growth and development of the story, taking over ownership and inquiry in their work. Finally they could celebrate their work through song, dance, story telling, iconography and enactment.

Taking material from other disciplines

Separate disciplines provide material for drama lessons, as well. A drama often takes its inspiration from **literature**, as the lesson samples in Part II readily illustrate. You'll find examples from The First Winter (in "Passage on the

Anne,") *Charlotte's Web*, *The Elephant's Child*, and Ghandi's autobiography. Working on a story in role tends to clarify it for the participants, providing ownership making it understandable and personal, and imprinting it deeply into the memory. Writing, reading and oral language experiences enrich drama lessons. They can be full of letter reading and writing, journal writing, reports and story making related to a central theme. Audio tape recorder and camcorder may augment the drama. In the living through of any group problem, it is a natural event for stories to be created and told, to make speeches, to discuss in small groups. Gibberish, foreign phrases, formal and informal language may all enhance drama lessons. In the world of theatre, grammar, syntax, diction and nonverbal communications all have a part to play.

Inspiration for lessons can come from the social sciences. **History** is a natural topic for the drama. One only needs to think about how Shakespeare turned to history for the basis of his dramas to realize how history offers a vast panorama of choices to the drama leader. Both theatre and history are basically about putting oneself in another's shoes. The historian and the actor both say, "There have been people like this, and I know them. Examples of historical dramas found in this text are "The Potawatomis of Pearline," "Indian Salt Belongs to India," "Passage on the Anne," "In the Land of the Kish" and "Oregon or Bust."

Drama always takes place within society; in fact, drama is one of the methods civilization has invented to examine society at the same time that it amused that very society. **Social science** topics that may be considered are politics, law, criminal justice, city, village, town, ethnicity and the family. Heathcote has been very successful in basing dramas on anthropology. She finds that anthropology distances classes from the immediate action of the times studied in a way that a history lesson cannot.

Much like anthropology, **science** can provide the content for the drama. Although it must be emphasized once again that the drama method is not very good at teaching facts, educational theatre can follow the scientific method and give a healthy respect for those engaged in scientific endeavors. Perhaps drama about space will be the most popular science topic with children, but in my experience young people also have great interest in human disease, zoology, and botany. Natural phenomena such as volcanos and floods have appeal. Although the drama may not be the best method to pass on scientific facts, research can be integrated into these lessons, or it can follow while interest is still high. There may have to be considerable distancing and symbolizing in working with science.

Art, dance and **music** should be a part of most drama classes. The arts can flow out of the drama naturally. Music appears as it would in life. In the Potawatomi lessons, art helped the children explain themselves with the schematics of wolf traps. It built belief through drawing the garden, bonded characters through artifacts, and moved the plot with crafts made for the treaty conference.

5

Attitudes, too, may be taught through thematic drama. I recently received a Michigan Generation Grant to use drama as a way to introduce students from a Latino neighborhood to begin viewing themselves as agents for change. In this semester-long project, sixty sixth grade students from an inner city elementary school worked with university students and community agencies to understand the workings, services, and joy of non-profit community leadership.

The sixth graders worked in groups of ten with student leaders on problems that arise from natural disasters. The work had begun soon after the California earthquake of 1994, and that provided the theme that interested four groups. They worked on the immediate problem of saving people who were trapped, then skipped ahead and did sessions on preparing a community for disaster. One group made a video of what had happened. This gave them an opportunity to think deeply about how people behave in disasters. Another group presented a rock concert to raise money for a disaster relief fund, and a third made masks to symbolize the emotions they felt about losing their schools and rebuilding a new one.

Of the two groups who decided not to use the earthquake, one played skiers lost in the Alps. This group's drama revolved around whether to help others in trouble or to get oneself out of a dangerous situation and forget the others. The last group took a story about a fire in Mexico where student firefighters only 14 years old were sent into a dangerous situation and died in a back-fire. That drama centered on mourning for the dead and then trying to bring the fire chief to justice. The teachers commented on how much good problem-solving and helping behavior they saw in these students. Since language was a barrier for some of them, the teachers were delighted to see English speakers cooperating with Spanish speakers, and Spanish speakers forgetting their self-consciousness and using more English as they worked in the drama.

Thematic drama works across the curriculum

Working in role gives an integated and spontaneous approach to learning. In working thematically the leader does not say, "Now we will learn history," or "Now we will learn art." The learning is so life-like that students do not have to ask, "Why are we learning that?" On the other hand, teachers may have to teach "the curriculum," whether children are interested or not. For example, teachers may have to create a play store at the second grade, even if the children are bored with playing store. This may be a problem for a teacher not trained to work thematically. But by using the suggestions found in this book an instructor may see how she can create a store that is not only a place to buy and sell, but an exciting environment where children may encounter poor people, a heart attack victim, naughty children, bankruptcy, robbery, a fire, an earthquake, a scandal about bad food, and/or a plague of mice. Someone can win a dream vacation in a prize drawing, or the owners can face great struggles as they reclaim their goods from a flood. It can be a place where criminals are given a second chance. The store is never "just playing store." There is little in the curriculum that is impossible to integrate and make exciting through drama.

Theatre is a way for player to know about the world holistically, using their intuition and making syntheses to problem-solve. Theatre is the opposite process to the logical step-by-step answer to questions that most education follows. Theatre is a way to explore subjects using all of the intelligences: logical/mathematical, spatial, musical, linguistic, kinesthetic, and inter- and intrapersonal. Teaching in role thematically comes to grips with education in an all-encompassing way that is interesting to the child and reflects the real world. In the Potawatomi lesson, for instance, it is clear to see that health, art, science, geography, music, dance and history were all integrated into one series of lessons. To paraphrase the words of the American teacher and philsopher John Dewey, the drama works with the whole child.

Recently the American Alliance for Theatre and Education has been engaged in a nation-wide research project aimed at definining theatre literacy and discovering how it is achieved. One of the findings shows that young learners view theatre a viable art form if they perceive it to be a way to express their own interests. Those who who perceive theatre as only an activity with difficult techniques to master, where someone else's ideas are expressed, look upon theatre as meaningless to their lives.

Thematic drama by its very nature is a reflection of the learners' interests and lives. In this style of drama, leaders and players strive for a deep level of involvement with constant internal analysis. The drama is open-ended, so the group is not being hurried to a pre-conceived conclusion. All arts can be incorporated in the style. No matter the content, thematic drama is always about how people live together, their joys and and struggles. Emotional moments are celebrated. The method respects the player's intelligence and accepts his or her feelings.

Theatre has been called a "way to make meaning." Pre-schoolers who do not understand an event in their life play it out, and it comes to have meaning for them. A young professional actress said of working in a performance art event with me, "I didn't understand when you were explaining the method of performance or how our actions related to the story, but when I was doing it, suddenly I understood."

What makes a good thematic drama leader?

A skilled drama leader thinks like a theatre artist. He or she must view life as a drama, seeing the possibilities of action, character and place. Leaders must develop the skill of concentration — living in the here and now in a persona different from their own. They must not be distracted by irrelevant details or let the actions of the other players alter their moods. For the beginning leader there is the temptation to laugh at young people's ideas and ways. But if adults are to have a full invitation to join youth at play, they must be able to resist any response that would make a young person feel inadequate.

The leader must enjoy taking a risk . . . be willing to fail as well as to succeed. Leaders must have a great curiosity about what will happen next. To succeed as a leader, you must be able to think on your feet. You must be willing to discover more about new places, new things, and even new information about yourself. You must not take yourself too seriously, but be willing to laugh at yourself and admit mistakes. Joy in life and a sense of humor will help immensely.

Sources

BOLTON, GAVIN. *Drama as Education: an Argument for Placing Drama at the Centre of the Curriculum.* Burnt Mill Harrow, Essex: Longman, 1984.

_____. *Towards a Theory of Drama in Education.* London: Longman, 1978.

COURTNEY, RICHARD. "Drama as a Generic Skill." *Youth Theatre Journal.* Summer, 1986. 1:1, pp. 5 through 11.

_____. "The Dramatic Metaphor and Learning," in *Creative Drama in a Developmental Context.* New York: University Press of America, 1985, p. 39 through 64.

DAVIES, GEOFF. *Practical Primary Drama.* London: Heinemann, 1983.

DAVIS, JED H. and TOM GEHM. "Terminology of Drama/Theatre with and for Children. A Redefinition." *Children's Theatre Review.* 37:1 (1978), pp. 10 through 11.

GARDNER, HOWARD. *Frames of Mind.* New York: Basic Books, 1983.

HEATHCOTE, DOROTHY. Lecture. Newcastle University, Newcastle-Upon-Tyne, England, September 7, 1985.

HEINIG, RUTH BEALL. *Creative Drama for the Classroom Teacher.* 3rd ed. Englewood Cliffs, NJ: Prentice Hall, 1988.

HERRIOT, JAMES. *Only One Woof.* New York: St. Martin's Press, 1993.

JOHNSON, LIZ and CECILY O'NEILL. *Dorthy Heathcote: Collected Writing on Education and Drama.* London: Hutchinson, 1984.

KOVALIC, SUSAN with KAREN OLSEN. *ITI: The Model: Integrated Thematic Instruction* 2nd Ed. Oak Creek, AZ: Books for Educators, 1993.

National Standards for Arts Education: What Every Young American Should Know And be Able to do in the Arts. Reston; MENC Publications, 1994.

O'NEILL, CECILY, ALAN LAMBERT, ROSEMARY LINNELL, and JANET WARR-WOOD. *Drama Guidelines*. London: Heinemann Educational Books, 1976.

_____ and ALAN LAMBERT. *Drama Structures: A Practical Handbook for Teachers*. London: Hutchinson, 1982.

Theory Into Practice: Educating Through Drama. Ohio State University, School of Education. 24:3 (Summer), 1985.

WAGNER, BETTY JANE. *Dorothy Heathcote: Drama as a Learning Medium*. Washington, D.C.: National Education Association, 1976.

Since Dorothy Heathcote wrote little herself, I took copious notes whenever I saw her in action at workshops and demonstrations, and in the videos she made for the B.B.C. and Northwestern University. I repeated these notes to my students so often they took on a quality of being my own.

In the late 1980's, Cecily O'Neill came to the U.S. to teach at Ohio State University. Through her visits to Grand Valley State University and a joint residency at the Attic Theatre in Detroit, I was able to know her and her work personally.

THINKING THEATRICALLY:
THE ELEMENTS OF DRAMA

"A drama class should do its thinking in its medium."

Dorothy Heathcote

This chapter introduces

• *drama as a teaching tool through the ages*

• *the basic elements of all drama*

• *an example of using these elements in thematic drama.*

IT IS SUMMER, AND TWO GROUPS OF THIRD AND FOURTH GRADERS purposefully run back and forth to the blackboard. The groups do not seem to speak English or understand each other for that matter. The studio light is dim, but the observer can just make out the two groups trying to send messages back and forth through pictographs. Aha! A breakthrough. They understood. Someone is sick; and in the other group, someone is a doctor.

In a darkened museum classroom six and seven year olds quietly and seriously move other players into poses of Egyptian statuary. A particularly shy boy who has stood off to one side now comes forth. As the museum inspector he makes delicate changes in the figures. His hands clap slowly and the statues come to life.

In a fifth grade classroom in a suburban school half of the class wave their arms in an animated fashion. They are successful politicians giving advice to a partner who is playing a teenage son or daughter. The "teenagers" have just announced that they intend to follow in their famous parent's footsteps. How will the "adults" advise them?

In a junior high school, pairs of students hastily sketch plans for a compelling picture they propose to put on the cover of next month's Parent's Magazine exploring the question, "Today's Parents: Good or Bad?" They move to the front of the room where the pictures come to life.

In a TV studio on a college campus, high school students move in and out of a tableau portraying the dynamic qualities of Rosa Parks' refusal to move to the rear of the bus in Montgomery, Alabama.

In a hushed basement drama room of an inner city high school, teenagers playing members of a city commission to fight crack in that city, share in role the ways that drugs have made their lives difficult and sad.

In a college classroom, men and women playing friends of a presidential candidate argue heatedly over whether they should or should not reveal her secret birth outside the U.S.A. to the media, or even to the candidate herself.

Actual scenes from thematic work, these dramas were able to explore some of life's most grippingly beautiful and touching moments. They celebrated heroes, wept with victims, and recognized the foibles of human kind with laughter. These scenes once again confirm Shakespeare's observation, "All the world's a stage and all the men and women merely players."

Drama as a teaching tool through the ages

From the time of the Roman critic Horace in 20 B.C., to television studies reported last week, drama has been recognized as a powerful teaching tool. Through the ages, young people have partaken in the theatre. They learned religious and church history during the great medieval church mystery plays which taught Bible stories and the lives of the saints to the illiterate masses. In Elizabethan England, children and youth were both audience members and actors in the theatre. France's Louis XIII as a child performed for a court farce, and at age seven he acted more and more in the theatre. In a French convent school a century later, Madame de Genlis taught her young wards informal drama. As an art form and as a method for learning, theatre continues to be a living tradition for young people in the school and community worldwide.

This book introduces thematic drama as a modern style that only adds to the long tradition of using the theatre as a valid teaching tool for our times.

Theatre, like all other arts, reflects and provides a structure for changes in our lives. Pre-schoolers use their own drama, social pretend play, to help them integrate new ideas and experiences into their understanding, and to interact with their friends. Theatre can do the same for any of us at any age. It furnishes a way to reflect and to share with people we enjoy. Like writing a love letter, or telling a side splitting story, it provides a forum for us to understand our lives better and to absorb experiences that enrich and amaze us. Play is the basis of human learning, and it is a natural form for the expression of joy and sorrow.

The basic structure of drama

One of the first steps for a future drama leader is to become familiar with many great dramas of the world. As examples for reference in this book, I've chosen *Romeo and Juliet* by William Shakespeare, Thornton Wilder's *Our Town*, Alain Boulin and Claude-Michel Schonberg's *Les Miserables*, and August Wilson's 1987 Pulitzer Prize-winng play, *Fences*. They will be used to illustrate the points discussed here.

Theatre is an art form as well as a method of learning. As any art form, it has aesthetics, theories and a vocabulary to be mastered. These are not difficult, but a grasp of them is essential in order to plan and execute successful work in the thematic style of drama. A beginning thematic drama leader needs to understand the basic structure of all drama.

For the purposes of leading drama, theatre has four central elements: playable action, character, environment and thought.

Playable action

Briefly, playable action is what happens in drama. Story in the theatre must not just be told. It must be acted out to be seen. Playable action is human interaction and explored relationships. It is not internal action or action so subtle that it cannot be seen in a classroom or on stage. "Show it, don't tell it," is a caution going back to Viola Spolin, mother of modern improvisation. The challenge in developing playable action is how to present a conflict between characters and groups so observers can see and make up their own minds.

Plot falls within playable action. But it suggests a more complicated relationship than narrative. It is the examination of how one event will cause another to happen. A sample narrative would be, "The king died and then the queen died." A sample plot would be, "The king died and the queen died of grief." To illustrate how cause and effect work in a play, imagine a scene in which a boy enters a room and slams a door. The slam causes the mother to scream at him. The scream then causes the boy to run away with a friend. Leaving home causes more action. Therefore plot refers to how one event causes another to occur.

In *Our Town*, George has been ignoring Emily because it is baseball season and his team needs his talent. This causes her to reprimand him and express her hurt. This in turn causes George to ask if she wants a soda. This causes her to have a serious talk to him, which in turn causes him to propose. And on and on. The philosopher Aristotle, who wrote about the art of theatre over two thousand years ago, considered this plotting of cause and effect the most important aspect of drama. This may be because moral growth seems to depend on an understanding of how the actions of one human being cause further actions in other human beings.

Playable dramatic action centers around conflict, or **tensions**. Experts claim that all drama can be classified into a small number of conflicts:

The hero vs. a villain — *Romeo and Juliet*
The hero vs. society — *Les Miserables*
The hero vs. nature — *Our Town*
The hero vs. himself — *Fences*

Stanislavski, the great twentieth century Russian drama teacher, pointed out that the element that made the drama interesting was the exploration of the lives of characters whose goals are thwarted, creating tensions so great, that the characters often are willing to risk their lives for what they believe, desire and need.

Dramatic tensions usually are caused by human emotions such as jealousy, greed, sacrifice and unrequited love. In *Romeo and Juliet*, Romeo must choose between his parents and his beloved. The tensions of this play grow out of such emotions as fear, love, jealousy, and desperation. The tension of *Fences* comes especially out of fear and jealousy. In *The Ice Wolf*, a play about prejudice based on skin color, Anatou's parents are in conflict with the other villagers. The tensions of the play are set in motion by fear, hunger, loss, and hatred. In the Potawatomi drama, the major tension lies between two groups of people without power distrusting each other. The hero in tension with society, or even a collective hero in tension with society provides a situation that can easily be adapted to use in thematic drama, because these situations concern conflicts that interest people, and they provide roles for many players.

Aristotle admired plots that had **reversals of fortune** for the leading characters. Today we still praise dramas that have extreme changes of fortune for characters, where the mighty are brought low, and the lowly raised. In Romeo and Juliet, the heroine goes from being a carefree teenager to a woman willing and able to destroy herself for love. *Les Miserables'* Jean Valjean goes from being a selfish, troubled young man to a deep-feeling, sensitive mature person willing to sacrifice himself for others.

Exciting playable actions also include **recognitions**. Characters often wear disguises, as they do in the masked ball in *Romeo and Juliet*. They disguise their own inner qualities or those of other characters. Troy in *Fences* fails to see himself repeating his father's mistakes. Self recognition of inner qualities within a character also makes up an important part of a plot. During the course of a piece, a character's true nature may be exposed; strangers may prove to be lost loved ones; the villain may prove to be a hero. Recognitions and reversals provide much of the excitement, surprise and suspense in the theatre.

Epic drama

Despite the fact that plot is so important to western drama, most of the drama from other parts of the world and much of twentieth century western drama's playable action is not plot based, but presented in an epic style. *Les Miserables* provides an example of this structure. Epics tend to have loose flowing action that skips from time to time and place to place, much as movies evolve. Western twentieth century epic theatre was developed by the German playwright Bertold Brecht. He replaced the frivolous emotion and entertainment that dominated the German stage of the 1930's with a drama that emphasized serious political questions and social problems.

Brech's "Epic Theatre" attempts to "distance" the action of a tale, making it strange. It cools the emotional involvement by stopping and starting the action, by having a narrator comment on the action, or having the actor comment on the action himself. It inserts songs, choral reading and poems that stop the action. It offers several possible endings. It includes more debate and less sentiment.

Although *Les Miserables* is social in theme, it has a sentimental treatment of character and highy emotional story and environment, which moves it away from Brecht's sense of distancing. But whatever the epic's individual differences, it is important for drama leaders to recognize this alternative theatrical style and study its structure, for epic theatre lends itself as well to thematic drama as classic structure does. Examples can be seen in "Indian Salt for Indians," "The House of Christine," and "The Elephant's Child."

The great dramas of the world provide an endless number of playable actions appropriate to explore in thematic drama lessons. Although the drama leader may not wish to recreate an entire classic drama, plots and sub-plots with their various tensions may be borrowed and liberally modified.

Character

No matter what the style of action, the story needs a hero who is pitted against a villain. Character works hand in hand with plot, in that the actions of characters grow out of plot and character grows out of action.

The term character may seem fairly self-explanatory. Most dramas are peopled by characters whose story the plot tells. But it is not only necessary to have people in a drama; those people must have "character" — principles, values, and motives that can be analyzed and examined. Much of what drama is about is the relationship between characters, how one character influences others' lives negatively and positively.

August Wilson's *Fences* illustrates the possibility of developing a deeply complex character. His hero, Troy Maxson, is driven by a host of conflicting emotions and circumstances. Troy is full of vigor, anger, hurt, searching, tenderness and cruelty. Although he is a man who feels deeply for himself, he cannot seem to reach out to others and feel with them. He only sees his own sacrifice and blames others for his problems. Troy's love for his tiny daughter does soften him, though. His great spirit coupled with his vulnerability, in search for what is right and just, no matter how warped his ideas, makes him worthy of our love and respect. In the end the fences fall as his family forgives him, and they move on with their lives.

Plays have protagonists (the heroes) and antagonists (the villains). Throughout the history of theatre, other characters have developed. A sampling of stock characters includes bragging soldiers, befuddled academics, rich, worried fathers, ingenues (romantic young women), leading men and leading women, second men and women, and so on. Cosette is the ingenue in *Les Miserables*, and Eponine the second woman. Stock characters provide a kind of shorthand to get an audience involved in a drama rapidly. They need not explain themselves in detail, thus leaving more time for the action and the thought of the piece.

Often there is a wise servant, as the nurse in *Romeo and Juliet*. This role may be a minor one, but it is one which gives added depth to the drama. It provides for some comic relief, gives other characters a sounding board, and provides the voice of experience. In thematic drama, a leader often plays this role.

Twentieth century plays often have narrators, such as the Stage Manager in *Our Town*. A narrator helps move the story and grounds the audience throughout the chaos of an epic drama. The leader may want to create stock roles for some players in the dramas he or she develops. Character will be a central concern for the teacher in planning thematic drama lessons.

Spectacle

Plays exist in time and place. They are of the here and now, not yesterday or tomorrow. They have a living out quality. The season, the ebb and flow of a lifetime, the rhythm of walking and speaking and all other aspects of time, therefore, are important to any drama. Theatre can not be repeated mechanically or electronically like a film or video. Much of the value of the theatre lies in the fact that time is precious, and the lives of the players who sacrifice time and talent for the audience, and the lives of the audience who sacrifice time and money for the event, will never meet again at this point where they are here and now. These valuable rhythmic aspects of life often are expressed in the rising and falling action of the plot and the dynamics of the piece: loud/soft, slow/fast, and up/down. Repetitions in threes provide rhythm, mystery and wonder. We know that music in one form or another has been important in the theatre from the beginning. In our illustrative plays, music is of utmost importance in *Les Miserables* and a central emphasis in *Our Town* and *Fences*.

Drama has often been called a metaphor which mirrors life. Like all other arts it is rich in symbolism. Symbols and metaphor can be found not only in the language of the play, but in its physical aspects as well. The props, the costumes, the mask, the makeup — all have a meaning far deeper than mere decoration.

Unlike literature which exists only in our imaginations, the theatre is tangible. It has a place to perform and bodies of flesh and blood to perform the actions. Environment includes sets, props, costumes and all of the parts of the play that appeal to the senses. Shakespeare's plays are full of spectacle: the ballroom, the balcony and garden, the tomb in *Romeo and Juliet*. Modern playwrights love spectacle, too, as seen in the wedding and funeral procession found in *Our Town* and the war scenes in *Les Miserables*.

Contemporary playwrights use spectacle as a way to enrich dramatic events and messages symbolically and nonverbally. Often spectacle accompanies recognitions and reversals, heightening them and making them more important. This can be no better illustrated than in the wonderfully complex revolving stage in *Les Miserables*. Performance art, which often has a totally nonverbal way of creating theatre, has an important place in theatre work with young people.

Theatre, however, can be meaningful and beautiful when it is sparse. Less can be more. A taste for an unembellish "poor" theatre developed in the 1970's. Lope de Vega, the great dramatist of Spain's golden age, said that all that is necessary for the theatre is a board (a space) and a passion (acting). Thematic theatre often reflects this lean quality. In work with young people, there is rarely the staff and financial support to include complex spectacle. The classroom is the place and two or three simple props provide the sensory elements. Beauty is found in the truthfulness of emotion, thought, and character.

Thought

Finally, Aristotle found that thought was an important element of the drama. This term may seem strange to us, but it may seem more familiar if we think about thought as relating to theme or even the moral of the play. "Thought" is really a better word, though, for unlike more modern terms, thought is all encompassing. Good plays have thought, and so do good thematic drama lessons.

Applying the theatre basics to a thematic drama

Some readers may be wondering how this structural description of theatre applies to a teacher working in a classroom with children. But structure will ground the drama leader in the work. Soon he or she will understand how to manipulate dramatic action, character, environment and thought. As he gains more theatre experiences, he will recognize the value of time, music, space, metaphor, and distance.

Here is an example of the way the elements of dramatic structure went into the planning I did for a lesson based on Kipling's "The Elephant's Child" from *The Jungle Book*. I planned this for a fairly typical group of second graders.

To begin, I wanted to apply all of the elements — playable action, character, spectacle and thought - to the story that formed the basis of the lesson. There is no one order in which a dramatic leader should attack this project, but all the inter-related theatrical elements have to be considered in course. Here I decided to begin with **thought**.

I first examined the basic themes in the story. I found curiosity, disobedience, friendship and helping, revenge, smugness, corporal punishment, power, making do, imagination and nonsense. A leader might want to play all of these themes, but I will select only one. In choosing particular themes to play, the leader must consider which ones complement the needs of a particular group of students. Age, temperament, space, interest and other variables would have to be considered. For example, with a group of timid children who feared taking risks, it might be desirable to use the theme of curiosity. The theme of nonsense could be celebrated with any group that could appreciate high-spirited fun without getting out of hand.

As a teacher, artist and human being, I would pick a theme that allowed me to feel comfortable and challenged. Surely I feel no need to celebrate the themes of violent spankings and retribution found in "The Elephant's Child." I also am not especially interested in the character relationship among the elephants early in the story. Themes that I enjoy and would like to explore further are nonsense, friendship, and making something good out of a thing which seems bad on the surface.

I then turn my attention to other elements of the drama to compare the structure of the short story with drama's structure and possible themes that I have isolated. As to **playable action**, a child (elephant) protagonist disobeys warnings and follows his own curiosity. In a dangerous encounter with the antagonist (crocodile) the hero and his wise companion (the python) survive. Because of the encounter, the hero experiences a positive reversal of fortune; and in the denouement he encourages society — that is, the other elephants — to conform to the change which his adventure thrust on him.

To further explore plot I asked myself a series of questions such as:

• Which of these causes and effects are most dramatic, and how can they be explored in informal theatre?

• What reversals and recognitions in the story call for attention?

• Are there incidents of playing the opposite, or disguises which would be interesting to explore?

Some actions in the original story which I see as piquing the interest for a group of second graders include:

• Spankings

• Being saved from a crocodile

• Going on an adventure with a friend, and

• Teaching someone a lesson.

We will leave these for now and move on to **character**. The major characters who appear in the story are the elephant child, the adult elephants, the crocodile, and the python. Not only are these animals characters, but they possess character. That is, they have a distinct set of values which determines right and wrong. The elephant's child is disobedient, but only because of his intellectual curiosity, which eventually proves to be of benefit to all elephants. The adult elephants, who never take an active place in the playing of the original story, are shown as brutes who spank at the slightest provocation. In an interesting dark twist, one of the most useful purposes the elephant child finds for the new trunk is as a means to return cruelty for cruelty. The python is a wise guide and friend for the small elephant in whose mouth philosophical comments are acceptable. As the antagonist, the crocodile is a danger but no life threat.

Poetic language abounds in Kipling's tale. Musical elements can be found in the poetic diction and repetition in plot which provides a ponderous but for-ward-moving rhythm to the journey to and from the water hole.

"The Elephant's Child" is rich is spectacle and dramatic action that would be exciting to perform and see. Included here are the tug of war over the nose, the trunk wrapped in banana leaves, and the actions the young elephant per-forms with his the new trunk.

Dramatic elements other than theme I decide to retain for their artistic impact are **repetitious language**, the **comic situations** dealing with a new trunk, and the **power of persuasion** the young elephant uses over his superi-ors. Now I must deal with the consideration, in planning this lesson, of how much to deviate from the original source.

The lesson begins to take shape

After entertaining these several considerations, I am ready to make some decisions on the lesson plan. In selecting the theme, I feel comfortable explor-ing "The Elephant's Child's" nonsense: the metamorphosis — the whimsical reaction and adjustment to a changed body part. This provides something to challenge me, too, as comedy is a difficult genre to use in the thematic mode, which normally deals in a serious, even tragic, world view. I now ask myself how I can devise a thoughtful and emotionally satisfactory drama.

The angle I choose to use with "The Elephant's Child" poses a comic point of view toward metamorphosis in self. Whereas the Kipling story has the ele-phant child get a trunk, I will place my class in a situation where they have just grown great huge ears, celebrating Kipling's wonderful sense of humor and a contemporary appreciate for the absurd. This angle is not only comic, but it explores the human condition by providing a parallel experience for bodily changes that are a part of growing up: growing taller than their classmates; reaching puberty, finding themselves pregnant or, at my age, losing hair.

(Recently I developed a metamorphosis with my back. At first I was dev-astated, worrying that I could never do my own decorating again, never take baskets of laundry outside to dry, never do this or never do that again. Then I began to see the advantages of having a bad back. I no longer had to carry bags of groceries up the hill from my garage to my kitchen. I no longer had to gath-er the garbage for the Monday morning pickup. If I could, I would talk all of you into having a bad back.)

This, then, is the point of view the class will explore: learning to like, hav-ing a sense of humor about, and even reveling in changes in self.

As in all other theatre, characters in thematic dramas must be in conflict, out of rhythm with environment, family, society, or self. Roles develop from these theatrical **tensions**. Young players prefer the role of protagonist or side-kick to the protagonist. Obvious roles that could be used in "The Elephant's Child" include all the characters in the story: the child himself, the python, the crocodile and the other elephants. In my plan I throw off all of these possibilities because personally, I do not like to ask people to be animals. It is another thing if players volunteer to be animals, but deep thematic work, even comedy, relies upon thought so much, that to be an animal may cancel thoughtful work, clouding the human condition rather than shedding light upon it.

The roles I choose for the players are to be themselves, a group of people who suddenly have ears the size of saucers. The **conflict** the characters grapple with is how to adjust to this unasked-for change. Should they get rid of the ears, adjust to them, ignore them, or use them and be proud of them?

A final aspect to be planned in a lesson is to discover an **inciting incident** that will arrest the attention of the group as it starts to work.

> (*Speaking awkwardly and hesitantly*) I woke up this morning, and there was this strange thing under my hair. First I felt it on the right side, and then, ahh, over on the left side. (Feeling) Do you see it? It's big and feels like skin or a bump and it kind of flops, and it, ah . . . Oh, Tammy, I didn't see that before, look at you. I think it has happened to you, too. Yours are kind of **big ears**. (*Apologizing*) Now they are pretty. I mean they're beautiful. In fact they look like lovely sea shells (*Pause*) — oooh, and they wave so gracefully in the air. Mine looks like that, too? (*Touching the imagined ears*) They do? Hmmm. Well, I wonder, yes, I do see that some of the rest of you have grown these big ears, too. Has everyone grown them?

From this point, the leader listens carefully to the group to find playable actions, improvising on the suggestions the group brings to the event. I think through some possible ways to continue ahead of time, so the drama will not have to skip a beat. These are possible activities to use after the opening words:

- Continue the discussion.
- Talk in pairs with a friend about the problems the huge ears create.
- The whole group could share innovative things to do with the big ears.
- Players could draw a picture of themselves with enormous ears.
- They could write a letter to someone about the problems the big ears are creating.
- Players could show in tableaux the uses of big ears.
- In round robin story-telling, or a liars' convention, they could explain how the ears got so big.
- The leader might host a talk show where the people with big ears are featured.

Even with these eight actions to choose from, a leader in touch with the spirit of the group might spontaneously come up with a ninth idea which would match the players and occasion better.

A final scene or point for the group to reach in this lesson or series of lessons may be planned. With the theme I have chosen here, I would want the group to arrive eventually at a point where they could convince another group — perhaps another second grade class, or half of their own class — that they, too, should grown big ears, because huge ears are useful and fun.

So, going into a thematic drama based on Kipling's "The Elephant's Child," I would have the following elements of drama ready to play:

- A **theme**: our body changes are significant in the comedy of life.

- **Characters**: we are ourselves, but we have changed.

- An inciting **incident**; Dr. Salazar discovers she has grown bulky ears.

- **A second step**: characters communicate feelings about their new conditions.

- A **conclusion**: everyone can learn to love their tremendous ears (life changes).

Sources

ARIES, PHILIPPE. *Centuries of Childhood.* T. Robert Baldick. New York: Knopf, 1965.

ARISTOTLE. *On Poetry and Style*, tr. G.M.A. Grube. New York: Bobbs Merrill, 1958

BOUBLIN, ALAIN and CLAUDE-MICHEL SCHONBERG. *Les Miserables.* London: Exallshow Ltd., 1990.

ESSLIN, MARTIN. BRECHT: *The Man and his Work.* New York: Doubleday & Co., 1960.

HORACE. "Horace: The Art of Poetry." in Bernard F. Dukor's *Dramatic Theory and Criticism.* New York: Holt, Rinehart and Winston, Inc., 1974. pp. 67 through 76.

KIPLING, RUDYARD. *The Elephant's Child.* Garden City, New York: Garden City Publishing Company, Inc. 1942.

KRAUS, JOANNA. *The Ice Wolf.* Charlottesville, VA: New Plays. 1963.

SALAZAR, LAURA GARDNER. ""The Emergence of Children's Theatre and Drama." Unpublished Ph. D. Dissertation, University of Michigan, 1984.

STANISLAVSKI, CONSTANTIN, tr. Elizabeth Reynolds Hapgood. *An Actor Prepares.* New York, Theatre Arts Books, 1948.

WILDER, THORTON. *Our Town.* New York: Harper, 1957.

WILSON, AUGUST. *Fences.* New York: Peguin, 1986

SOME BASICS OF THEMATIC DRAMA

*"Drama gives depth. It takes a microcosm
and exposes it."*
Dorothy Heathcote

This chapter introduces

• *finding meaning through doing;*

• *segmenting;*

• *the "brotherhoods; and*

• *setting goals.*

PLAY IS A NATURAL STATE FOR YOUNG CHILDREN. Thematic drama relates to, but differs from play. It is no mere coincidence that the word for what children do with their time, and the adult dramatic vehicle have the same English word, play. All healthy children play, and, as Piaget has pointed out, it is the way that children learn. Through trying on roles and emotions they master their environment. The research of Loren Barritt and his Dutch colleagues indicate that children like to play in private, and to play rather "naughty" games, far away from disapproving adults. The leader of thematic drama needs to keep these characteristics of play in mind when developing scenarios for play.

Although creative drama is based on play, it is not to be confused with natural play itself. Creative drama leaders take the natural impulse to play and frame it through subject matter and problem solving. They add the component of reflection, restructing time in the story and in the day. They provide the banks through which the stream of play may flow.

There is no formula for how to lead drama. Theatre is an art, and like all arts, it is expressed in great variables. A broad range of possibilities exists, and what appears in this book or any book on the subject only sketches in the barest essentials. Every theatre leader must develop his or her own style, the same way that each writer develops an individual voice or a painter develops a recognizable use of color and line. Although there is no formula for thematic theatre, it moves from a set of basic assumptions. These will be discussed in this chapter.

What is different about teaching in role

In role, the teacher stops teaching about a subject, and with the class explores and becomes the subject. In a drama lesson based on a science content, the class would become a team of experts called in to examine a failure of banana trees to thrive on a tropical island. Students use the scientific method to solve the problem. They do not use someone else's answers. In order to plan and carry out the work realistically, the teacher may have to learn a great deal about tropical plants and how to set up a variety of experiments; but this will be an appropriate use of the teacher's training and will teach players what science is really about.

Thematic theatre does not use a script, so the leader must create a scenario improvisationally with the group. Exploring human problems and developing new dramatic forms for the exploration makes teaching creative, exciting and fun. It also makes it hard work. But ideas for stimulating theatre are everywhere, and with a solid understanding of structure, creating lessons becomes easier.

A beloved story can be used over and over again to explore its many themes. Informal drama is more centered on the process the group follows than where the lesson ends. Our Town could be used for exploration of teen life at the turn of the century, its themes of longing for far away places, its unique presentation of immortality, its view of small town life.

Heathcote worked every morning for twelve weeks with some five-year olds, exploring the theme of King Arthur. They addressed the problem, "What do knights do when they are not in battle?" Twelve-year-olds working with the same material asked how strangers could tell who a person was by what was worn or the identity of a knight from the shield he carried. "How does it feel to spend the first twenty years of your life with the pigs and then become a king?" was the question from the Arthurian legend that fifteen-year-olds examined in the drama.

"Segmenting"

No drama lesson can explore everything about a subject. It is the leader's job to guide the group, to be selective, using organizational skills while the process is going on. It is also his job to help the class select a manageable chunk of a subject to deal with, often thinking on one's feet. All people have similar needs, and achieving any of these needs provides interesting tensions that can form the basis for dramatic work. Any third grader can come up with a respectable list of the needs of all people in all places. One young group can up with the following list:

Food	Oxygen
Safety	Laws
Religion	Sleeping
Doctors	Families

Other items such as transportation and shelter could be added, but the ones the children chose worked nicely. Finding these various aspects is termed "segmenting." One day's work could not be given over to playing everything there is to know about pirates. But one could give over a day to working on some aspect of pirates. Perhaps, "How do pirates take care of themselves when they are sick?" Segmenting provides a small enough topic to give the drama focus. Under most circumstances, children should name a number of segments and choose from the list the ones they want to play. Choosing in this way provides a valuable device for empowering young people and ensuring their commitment to the work.

To expand on segmenting, I will use the example of a lesson on American people living near the Arctic Circle. Any of the needs of the people could be a chosen segment. From that segment the leader and students would begin to ask questions about the people's life. What do they do when there is a shortage of food? How do their laws clash when the laws of the land clash with those of tradition? What is it like to be in a school with only four other students and a teacher who does not speak your native tongue? How does the long dark winter affect people's moods? What gives the courage to these people to go far out on the ice to catch fish for their village?

How does the leader know when the lesson is over?

Often the clock on the wall determines when time is up, but this is not a satisfactory answer. English drama pioneer, Peter Slade, describes something he called "Child Time." It was his contention that children know when they want to stop, and nothing can make them go on if they feel that this is the end. A group of sixth graders tried their old queen (the author in role in "Land of the Kish") for conspiracy, and found her guilty. When I pointed out that they had put her through a very poorly planned trial, not even allowing her any defense, and with no real evidence, the class had no interest in reopening the proceedings. They were happy with the outcome. They decided that the queen was bad, and she needed to be punished; they were very smug about their way of disposing of her. The time for her to be saved was past and their conclusion provided closure for them.

On the other hand, not to continue when the players feel the drama is not completed leaves players dissatisfied. That occured in the "Oregon or Bust" lessons, when the oxen died. Likewise, the Potawatomi story never did reach a satisfactory conclusion. Far too many loose ends were left untied, and the group was not ready to end. As an example of finding a proper ending, the lesson "Indian Salt Belongs to India" came to a satisfactory close.

Slade noted that the good drama leader will look for clues from the children to indicate when the drama is over and when it must continue. Unfortunately, the drama specialist who must appear for class on a specific time and day such as 10:00 every Thursday morning for a 40-minute class cannot always work with this characteristic of childhood and creativity. A series of classes demands that the leader stop at a high point that will keep the player's curiosity up until the next week.

Finding the tensions

Players need to face serious problems with interesting conflicts. Conflict in drama is not the same as violence, or even what advertisements for television call "action." Rather it is a tension. It shows a hero out of synch with the rest of his world, a Juliet who will not marry someone "safe" whom her family approves, but rather the son of their greatest enemy. Most players, especially young ones, are not afraid of big problems; and they willingly take on the challenges of world peace, settling the west, reliving the Trojan War, and finding gold in Alaska. The problems of the great world dramas provide excellent subject matter for even young children. Handling conflicts improvisionally, however, calls for technique coupled with an understanding of dramatic structure.

The Russian director Stanislavski broke the scenes he directed into several levels of tensions. In order for a scene to work on stage, he said, there must be a tension related to the participants' interaction with each other. In addition, he insisted that there had to be a physical level of tension. He turns into "I wants" for each character. Here is an example of the "I wants" in a simple domestic scene:

A woman is discovered on stage washing dishes. She wants to straighten up the house. She turns off the radio. She washes very slowly. She also wants to have peace and quiet. Her husband arrives home inebriated. He wants to have his dinner. And he wants to tell her that he loves her. She then wants to tell him that she is going to leave him. She still wants to get the dishes done. He wants to eat his dinner. The phone rings; she answers it. It is her mother. She does not want her to know that there is trouble. She breaks a dish. She starts to cry. She does not want her husband to see the tears. He then starts to remember their child who has died. He wants her to reminisce with him. She does not want to think about this.

And on and on. Life, along with theatre, is a series of character "I wants," and when they are in conflict internally or between characters, interesting drama results.

In *Our Town*, Emily's major desire for the scene in the drugstore is reassurance that George feels for her as she feels for him. In addition to these, there are minor "I wants." Emily's "I wants" in that scene might be outlined as follows:

• I want to walk home.

• I want George to know that I'm disappointed in him.

• I want George to be perfect.

• I want him to like me.

• I don't want him to see me cry.

• I don't want the Stage Manager to hear what we are saying.

• I want to show George that I forgive him.

• I want George to know that "I am now. I always have been."

The leader must make sure that there are enough "I wants" in a scene, that they are realistic and interesting and symbolize something deeper than the physical.

The Brotherhoods

Dorothy Heathcote has said that "Drama is the ability to associate with other people." Players can identify with their roles to such a degree and have visceral experiences so intense that it changes their point of view about life. Heathcote termed this effect "The Brotherhoods." The brotherhoods leave the lasting impression with the players that they have joined all those others in history who have suffered sorrows and loss, thrilled with courage, sighed in hopeless love, or taken pride in a job well done. Heathcote believes these dramatic experiences help people, young and old alike, realize that they are not alone in their life struggles. In addition, drama encourages them to reach out to others who are experiencing similar feelings and circumstances. Along with tension, the brotherhoods stand at the core of theatre as the central reason to engage in impersonation and mimesis, the characteristic which makes the study of theatre truly a humanity.

A drama lesson should provide at least one strong brotherhood, and it may provide many more. It is desirable to take students into brotherhoods they have not experienced before, one that will stretch them as human beings. A lesson on "Beowulf" that I taught did just that. It forced the players to join the brotherhood of all who celebrate a great victory, all who cross the fen alone, all who face certain death. Weeks after the lesson, the players, students in an alternative high school, confirmed the theory by volunteering the information that they never look at a swamp without remembering that they too have crossed it with intense fear; never hear about an attack on an enemy without feeling the certain death that moves with the company, never attend an awards ceremony without feeling the thrill of pride in accomplishing the impossible.

The brotherhoods have proved to be practical. One study of altruism in the Nazi Holocaust noted that 48% of the people who saved Jews and others from the Nazis had theatre training of one sort or another. An important part of these heroes' personalities was the ability to identify intimately with the victims they saved. They developed the ability, through their dramatic experiences of moving, thinking and feeling like others, to identify with people who normally would have been alien to them.

Not only should young people identify with victims, but they also need to identify with those who are successful, happy, whole, victorious people, with Emily and George of *Our Town*, with Cosette of *Les Miserables*. Drama can provide the "trying on of character," as Winifred Ward, the pioneering leader of informal theatre for young people in the United States, described it.

Adults can benefit also. Teachers often suffer from great frustration and have poor self concepts. Providing experiences in drama which lift their spirits and give them a memory of success can be rewarding for them and their leaders. Through the subject matter for "The House of Christine," I chose to empower teachers enrolled in a summer school class by helping them identify with beauty, business acumen, and glamour. These brotherhoods helped the class grow in beauty and spirit.

When a group of college students worked on the project called "Oregon or Bust," they discovered these brotherhoods: all those who are not chosen; all who are chosen; all who wait; all who are hopeful for the future; all who make a new society; all who are in a clique; and all who face the unknown. In the lesson "Indian Salt Belongs to India," some of the planned brotherhoods were all who worry about a beloved person who is in danger, and all who decide to resist in a non-violent way.

It is not necessary to discuss the brotherhoods with the youngest of children, although third and fourth graders should be able to talk about them. By the time young players reach junior high school age they should be quite articulate about how they identified with the characters they encountered and played in the drama.

Although brotherhoods can be planned somewhat ahead of time, opportunities for new brotherhoods to explore will occur in the improvisation. The leader must be able to decide to explore or reject new brotherhood opportunities.

A balance of thought and action

All drama is a rhythm of action and thought. In planning a lesson it is necessary to keep in mind that the action of the drama is of value only if it leads to reflection. Often the best dramatic action is not action at all, but playable experiences that reside beside the biggest happenings. In a lesson about space travel, it may be best to play the drama out in the control room, rather than on the unknown planet or space ship itself. In ancient times the Greeks believed that violence was out of place on the stage. Their stages showed the palace gates where kings and queens reacted to the horrible things that were happening elsewhere. Nobody saw Medea kill her children; only their dead bodies were wheeled on stage.

A balance of action and thought leads to positive classroom control. If the lesson has too much action, there is the danger of the players losing focus. A possible set of rhythms for a lesson could be the following:

- Arrest the children's attention by telling the children that they will receive their character name today in the naming ceremony
- Plan and discuss what should be planted in Mrs. Allen's garden
- Crown Princess Sunflower (child instigated)
- Finish planning
- Prepare the land and plant the garden
- Reflect on the work to date
- Participate in the naming ceremony

- Reflect alone (sleep)
- Hear disturbing news from Mrs. Allen
- Kill Mrs. Allen

This was the rhythm of the second day of the Potawatomi lessons. It is interesting to consider the poeeibility that Mrs. Allen was "killed" because the earlier hours of the lesson had an overabundance of quiet planning. The players may have been lookng for some excitement, and it should have been provided in a less violent way. Further lessons in the Potawatomi series took the children's need for adventure more into account. Rhythms have to be selected during the playing out of the story. They are subtle and elusive. They call for close attention to the group.

Goals

In addition to the basic assumptions of thematic drama, there are some basics to planning for a specific lesson. Early in planning a lesson, a leader must consider the goals to be addressed in the work. There are three levels of goals working in any given drama lesson. The first is the **thought** or **content** goal. On this level, the drama teacher decides what brotherhoods, tensions, characters, human interaction, metaphors and the time and space will be explored. Curricular decisions should be stated in this goal. Will the lesson take as its content and/or context 19th century American history, volcanoes, the study of family living, or any other "required" course?

On the second level, there are **group** goals. Drama lessons provide opportunities to work in groups to solve problems. The leader designs the lesson so that the plays have experiences that will help the group work together — to develop inter- and intrapersonal intelligences.

On the third level, the leader plans the work to address the art of theatre: techniques, artistic decisions, history, theory and criticism. Some such **drama** goals might be to improve pantomime or to become acquainted with the characters in *Romeo and Juliet*; another might be to manipulate plot or to apply criteria to evaluate a tableau.

Plays — and goals — must be age-appropriate. As with literature, drama must relate to child development: interests and stages of physical, mental and moral growth. This can be learned through books, but drama leaders must also spend time with young people in order to understand them.

Leaders need to consider the amount of time it takes to achieve each goal. Will the group need one short lesson or many longer lessons? Drama uses time as its plaything. Often it stretches time, it repeats time, it skips over time. It may reach its goals through moving forward or backwards in time, shortening and lengthening as it goes. Posing big problems in interesting rhythms creates exciting dramatic works.

Questions for leaders to consider

It is important to think through and visualize every aspect of the drama. How can the lesson be electrifying and deep? Where might players be confused? Where might rowdy behavior or *double entendres* disrupt the play? Will the players be asked to do something the leader himself would not do?

The leader should never consider the option that the players have the freedom to participate or not, or that they have the choice to behave as if they are or are not the characters they play. It must be the leader's attitude and assumption that the players will concentrate and suspend disbelief as long as the group is in role. Yet lessons need not be stopped because players are unwilling or unable to suspend their disbelief. During every lesson players fall into and out of belief. Usually this causes no problem if it does not affect others' concentration in role.

Leaders need to consider how they want to introduce drama to the group. They need to consider the mechanics of group leadership. Will they use terms like "freeze" and "curtain" to stop and start the work? How will they introduce pantomime? How much background will they give the players about their goals and the theories of theatre? Will they jump into the drama immediately and let explanations follow? How will they allow flexibility for each group to develop its unique personality?

Roles that the leaders and players will assume are another area of concern. The role chosen by the leader must break the powerful student/teacher relationship. It must not be too "teacherly," too powerful. Leaders should consider playing a role that is rather befuddled, a person with a problem that the players have power to solve. In the Potawatomi sessions, the adults' roles emerged with far too much power. Because of this, the players continually looked to the leaders for the answers to their questions. Force and even murder became their only way to win against these authority figures.

Heathcote believes that in "Middle Rank Roles" the leader has the power to change the direction of the drama, but he is not so powerful as to threaten the players. In the drama of the Kish, it would have been much better if I had led the Kish people in a weaker role than that of the old princess. By contrast, as Mlle. DuBois in "The House of Christine," I was fairly helpless as a new person at the firm. Thus, the players felt confident to work on their design projects. The role of the head cook in "Prison at River's Bend" is another good example of a successful middle rank role. These middle rank roles are more comfortable for the beginner, too, because it is usually easier to believe someone closer to your own life experiences than someone glamorous, rich, powerful, or brilliant. An ideal role for the leader, regardless of the topic, is concerned citizen.

At the same time that the leader is at the middle rank, it is important for the players to be in the role of the experts. In "Old Charley," it is Jim's friends who know where he may be and what he may be doing, not the leader in the role as waiter. Heathcote calls this giving the "Mantle of the Expert." In the drama young people can be scientists, great musicians, and race car drivers. With this cloak of expertise, they can grapple with important problems that face the adult world. The leader who naturally wears the mantle of the expert in life must drop it for the time of the drama lesson.

It is probably a good thing not to have an ending in mind while in the planning stage. This keeps the drama fresh and more life-like. We go through life with the excitement of the unknown driving us. Heathcote reminds us that people take too bland a role when there is over-planning. Keeping the ending unknown provides a cutting edge. It moves the drama beyond role-playing and gives it the power of real life.

The element of language

Spoken language is a basic element of the drama. It is a great advantage for the creative drama leader to develop a variety of voices. Although some people have a natural talent for voices, others can develop them over the years. Leaders can practice by listening to foreign languages, speakers from afar, and tapes of their own speech. They should become attuned to the speech of younger and older people, rich and poorer people, and the sick and the well. Word choice as well, and pitch, timing, melody and volume need to be studied. One way to practice is get a group of friends and give puppet shows for each other using various voices.

One word of caution, however. Leaders should not display too much technique, or beginning players may be intimidated by what seem to them to be unattainable skills.

Gibberish is fun to learn, and it can be very useful to the drama leader. It is a series of made-up syllables that have no meaning. It emphasizes non-verbal aspects of communication such as gesture, vocal tones, pauses, facial expressions, and eye contact. The vocalization has to be rhythmic like real language (although not necessarily English). Thinking about the content of what is being said will put the equivalent emotion into the speaker's gibberish.

Even without prompting, young people are better at mimicking voices than adults. Players often fall into the use of gibberish to emulate a foreign language. In a drama lesson about a trip to a distant planet, the natives of that planet (a group of eighth grade girls) began to speak gibberish when a space ship from Earth landed. After the lesson they related that they were as surprised as the others in the group that they could do it. They had no intention of speaking gibberish until one began to do so. And to their amazement, they were able to communicate with it through non-verbal channels.

In a drama lesson, adults must talk to players, be they children or adults, as if they were all adults. Leaders must not talk down to the group. Young people can tell when leaders are not sincere. Sometimes librarians and elementary school teachers talk to children with a different voice than the one they use to talk to adults. The words are over-pronounced, the pitch is much more varied than the pitch used in adult conversation, and the rate is much slower. This unnatural voice indicates that the leader is unable to believe herself, and that the players do not need to be sincere in their belief, either. On the other hand, children have been found to listen better to a high-pitched voice, so the pitch is not part of the problem.

What about equipment?

Informal drama calls for little or no physical equipment. All that is absolutely necessary is an open place to work and emotional commitment. Technical elements bog down the drama with unnecessary spectacle. The only equipment recommended are rostrum blocks and a few simple props and costume pieces. Rostrum blocks are simple finished wooden boxes large enough for one or more persons to stand or sit upon. Usually they come in sets of four or five, in a variety of sizes. It is helpful if they can nest in each other. In the drama they become furniture and indicate place and importance.

Although it is not advisable to have many props, a drama lesson may call for one or two important props. One recent method of determining intelligence includes the ability to manipulate objects. Researchers have discovered that one central way that humans communicate is through artifacts. Child development specialists were not surprised to find that in a recent research project, even very young children fell into two groups of interest: those interested in other people, and those interested in objects. The use of props in drama provides those who have objects as a central interest with a way to participate.

All of the great dramas of the world have a few key objects. Could there be a *Romeo and Juliet* without the vial of poison? Or the horror of life and passion without Gabriel's trumpet in *Fences*? A few well-chosen props can become metaphors for characters and themes in drama. They add to the mood of a piece and provide powerful visual and tactile memories. Through the power of symbols, we experience life more deeply both on the stage and off.

Basic assumptions, then, that one may make about thematic drama are that

• It holds to the learner's pace;

• It uses the themes of great literature;

• It is founded on the suspension of disbelief;

• It teaches the brotherhoods;

• It is based on tension.

The basics of planning a lesson include inventing roles for the players and leaders, planning the happenings and the brotherhoods, touching action and thought, segmenting and time structure.

Sources

BARRITT, LOREN, TON BEEKMAN, HANS BLEEKER and KAREL MULDERIU, "The World Through Children's Eyes: Hide and Seek and Peekaboo." *Phenomenology and Pedagogy*, 1:2, 1983, pp. 140 through 161.

COLERIDGE, SAMUEL TAYLOR. "Biographia Literaria," *The Complete Works of Samuel Taylor Coleridege*, Vol. III. Ed. Professor Shedd. New York: Harper and Brother, 1858.

SALAZAR, LAURA GARDNER and GRETTA BERGHAMMER, VICTORIA BROWN and HOLLY GIFFIN. Social Pretend Play: Technical *Report Number 2*. Tempe, AZ: American Alliance for Theatre and Education, 1993.

SLADE, PETER. *Child Drama*. London: University of London Press, 1954.

SUSPENDING DISBELIEF AND
EXPLORING EMOTION

"Demand emotional as well as intellectual response in role."

Dorothy Heathcote

This chapter discusses

• *the role and power of emotion;*

• *techniques for suspending disbelief;*

• *and layers of belief.*

THE OPPORTUNITY TO EXPRESS STRONG EMOTION is one of the most important gifts that theatre has for an individual. Throughout history, theatre has provided a place to exercise the emotions as well as the intellect. Aristotle saw the presence of pity and fear with the purgation of the psyche that followed as the chief function of drama. Various ages of drama have provided audiences and participants lesser and greater amounts of emotion, but it has always been present.

Emotional expression is important in the late twentieth century when freeways, upward mobility, and the media hold others at a distance. Social sexual roles cause us to restrict our emotions to the point that we deny having them. For fear of ridicule, we refuse exposing our deepest selves to others, even those we love. When someone asks us how we feel, we say "fine." Not only is this a convention, but we may not be enough in touch with our emotions or others' emotions to give an honest answer.

Just as there are individuals who cannot express emotion, there are others who can not rein in their emotions. Since drama deals in both showing and controlling emotion, it can provide role models and practice in the healthy balance of expression and restraint.

One of the underlying goals of all drama lessons must be the exercise of the emotions. In most cases there cannot be emotion expressed without physical and emotional commitment to the moment. This commitment is belief. Unfortunately, young people learn early that they can be the subject of ridicule if they act in some way that contradicts the unattainable ideal that they think they see in their peers, fashion magazines, and on the television screen. They must be "cool" on every occasion. Young people who perform in drama as people younger than themselves may ask themselves, "If I act as one of the children in this play, will my friends think that I'm a baby?" How, then can we build belief, free the emotions, and exercise control?

Believing the "big lie"

The first step of any drama lesson may be the intellectual agreement of everyone involved that, for the time of the drama, the participants must will-

ingly suspend their disbelief. Heathcote calls this "believing the big lie."
While working in role, everyone must believe the lie together. The group
agreement makes the agreement that for now "we will behave as if. . . . "

For young children, the big lie can be presented by simply stating something
like, "Now we are going to imagine that we are in the land of the Wild Things."
For older groups, a brief word about the importance of everyone's cooperation
in belief will be enough at the beginning. The leader may tell the group that the
overriding rule of the drama game is to behave as if the imagined thing is really happening. By calling this "believing the big lie," the leader makes it clear
that she expects the participants to work at suspending disbelief.

Belief will not be accomplished in the opening moments for a lesson; it
must be attended to throughout the lesson, and therefore will naturally fade in
and out for leader and players alike during the course of the work.

For years there has been a debate as to whether the actor lives the part or
puts on a mask. Although the debate is interesting, it is as irrelevant for the
drama leader as it is for the actor, because great figures from the history of
world theatre have adhered to both philosophies and been successful.
Perhaps the best advice for the leader of creative drama is to keep in mind
the dual reality of being self and character in childhood play: being Sharon
and being Cinderella at the same time. No healthy child in play believes that
she is Cinderella. All of the time she is still aware that she is Sharon; but she
is trying on the role of Cinderella as she would put on a dress or coat, wear-
ing the character on her body and inside her mind to experience what it
would feel like.

Without leader belief there cannot be participant belief.

The leader must not deny a role non-verbally. That is, as a leader one cannot say one thing and deny it with a facial expression or body language.
Research shows that observers believe non-verbal communication over verbal communication when they contradict each other. In the university classroom I often see students talking gibberish about some serious subject, but
they are smiling broadly. Such a contradiction is called "leakage," and its
phoniness can easily be detected. Leakage often happens when we tell a lie,
especially one that we may feel strongly about or have guilty feelings about.
In leakage one part of the body may show tension or movements while other
parts seem under control.

Leakage is difficult to get rid of completely, but the less leakage, the better
actor one is considered. Here is an example. As a liturgist in my church I had
to read a verse from the Bible that contained a string of unfamiliar place names.
I got the reading ahead of time, and I practiced.

I was determined that I would get them right. There was more than a little
bit of my ego involved. On Sunday morning, I read them smoothly, with cor-

rect grammatical and literary intent and pronunciation. Afterwards, one of my friends came up to me and said, "Excellent job of pronouncing all those unfamiliar words, but I knew that you were nervous. Did you know that all through it you wiggled your fingers on your right hand?" My fingers provided the leakage that my friend successfully interpreted as a struggle.

Helping children build belief in role

For young children, falling into roles is as easy as eating or sleeping. But as children grow, more personality emerges, and they have a very strong identification with who they are. They feel insecure taking on a role other than the one they have developed for themselves. In early elementary school children also develop processes of self presentation and self-evaluation and begin to be able to see themselves as other see them. They become aware of social pressures which dictate that "pretend" is something that adults don't do very often, or under only very special circumstances. Few six-year-olds have inhibitions about falling into roles; almost all eleven-year-olds do. This means that in a group of children age 8 to 10, there will be some children who have passed into the age of adult belief, while some of the children are still at the younger level of role play. This is normal, but has to be dealt with in the theatre class.

Children want to address serious problems, and in their expanding self-awareness they have a deep desire for others to treat their ideas and identities seriously. The most genuine compliment an adult can pay a young person is to respect his or her ideas and to meet on equal ground.

It must be clear to the group as well as the leader that being in role is not being on stage. It is much safer to be in role. In role the actor is playing herself. No one is watching, and mistakes are allowed. Further, role is not really unfamiliar to the player. People play many roles in their lives. Every day I play several different roles: teacher, writer, scholar, wife, director, mother, citizen, boss, friend, and confidant. Each role may call for subtle changes in wardrobe, makeup, language, and posture. I slip easily from one to the other. We may then actually say that, like children, we are still playing roles; but they are subtler and fewer in number, because of place, character and other limiting factors in our lives.

Belief is much easier if the group believes together. Groups reflect the moods of their leaders. Above all, the leader must believe and enter into the action wholeheartedly. The leader must commit to the work physically, intellectually, and emotionally. She has to show a willing suspension of disbelief from the first minute of the work. Moods are contagious. and the group will pick up the high seriousness, the festive spirit, or the worry a leader portrays. The leader will also be affected by the group's mood, and often the spirit of the group can help the adult leader.

A word about watchers. It is essential that there be as little feeling of audience at a drama lesson as possible. The watchers are guests, and none-too-welcomed guests. They must behave as polite guests. Once, early in a semester, I had university students watching "Prison at River's Bend," and had not yet warned them that it was very poor manners — and pedagogy — to laugh at the children's serious attempts to cope with the problems the drama posed. How can the children hope to maintain their serious roles if they are the butt of adult laughter? Laughter by outsiders and leaders has the potential of either causing embarrassment or showing off, both conditions which work against absorption for the participants. Later, when I put the watchers to work, they jumped in and did very well in the participation — one as a prison janitor, others as a librarian, a news seller, and mothers of the prisoners.

Helping the leader build belief in role

It will help the leader to play off another believing adult. (See the chapter on Working with a Partner.) Much as the leader helps the children, another adult in role can give a needed change in mood. Anyone who has worked on stage will know that having a partner who is deeply concentrating on his part can move the first actor into the world of make believe. The actress playing Juliet can only be good if she has a sincere performer playing the nurse.

The hardest part of building belief for the leader may be the natural reluctance adults have to getting into role. The maturing and socialization process has made most adults inhibited about acting another character then themselves. The desire for pretending functions at all ages, but in most adults it has moved to the level of daydreams. In drama a leader with serious respect for her class can move student's daydreams out of their heads and into the drama room, no matter what the age of the participant. A future teacher commented to me recently that the experience of working in role affected her all day. Before the experience she had no idea how much power a role has over the player. The drama leader must pass on to classes respect for, and love of living through and trying on role. Further, a respected teacher who loves to play roles will be a great comfort to those children who may be worried that pretend is too babyish or girlish for them.

Much of actor training is designed to counteract learned inhibitions. Acting teachers use rituals and exercises to focus thought and energy on performance and character as the actor takes the stage. Some exercises for actors will be useful to the drama leader as she prepares to meet a class in role. These same exercises may also help mature groups who are reluctant to suspend disbelief.

Vulnerability

Although the theatre is sometimes about stunning technical feats, it is also about being vulnerable. When the leader and players show each other that they both are human, trust and belief deepen; vulnerability, as much as strength, builds a sense of group. Several years ago I taught in an Upward Bound program. As they went about the motions of rehearsal for a formal play, the

African American high schools students showed that they really didn't trust a white teacher. On the day of the first and only dress rehearsal I was informed that the theatre would be unavailable for our work. At that point, I broke down and cried, because I really believed in the play and in the students. I knew that without that rehearsal we would not have a good show. My display of sincere emotion so moved the players that once we got in the theatre, they rehearsed twice as hard as before, and performed very well. In addition to that, they became my friends, and defended me when unknown students taunted me as I walked by. Vulnerability can be a very endearing trait, as the chart of Gibb's supportive behaviors on page 48 shows.

When I partnered in a class with publisher Patricia Whitton, she confessed that she was nervous about teaching in role for the first time. I said, "Oh, it will be fine!" Then she asked me what I would do. I told her I planned to tell a story about landing our spaceship on earth after a one-hundred hear journey. As I told her, I used several wrong terms, stuttering and bobbling. We both laughed and agreed that I was as nervous as she. I was determined to use my vulnerability, and when it came time to tell the story, I put all the fear I had of the present situation into my fear of landing back on Earth after all those years. The results provided a highly emotionally charged beginning to the lesson — I had found a way to use my vulnerability for my art.

The place of props in building belief

Interestingly enough, costumes and props usually help adults in role. Adults take out some of their nervous energy on a prop, as handling the object tends to burn up excess adrenaline. It also give focus to their work. When planning a lesson, leaders may want to think about a prop that may help them feel the role. This could be a cane, a jacket, a hat, a letter. Adults often communicate who they are through artifacts. That is one reason it is so hard for the elderly to give up their homes and cars: for them it is like losing who they are.

Props often hinder belief for children, however. For young people a real prop can become something to show off with, even to throw, or to "fool around" with, thus killing belief. A complex real prop such as a weaving loom will emphasize children's incompetence. With such props, they become frustrated at their inability to make adult manipulations; and this frustration destroys belief. Imagined props give children mastery.

Psychologist John Klimo has pointed out the value of manipulating objects for the development of the brain. It may prove that the use of props have a very important part to play in the developmental aspects of educational drama. Heathcote thinks some scholar needs to study the symbolic power of properties. Although she does not use many props, she suggests that an essential prop as symbol may be discovered and used to develop moods such as awe. As an example, she tells how in one lesson a ring for a bull's nose became a perfect symbol of brutality and unbridled anger. The Potawatomi tribe came to value their garden so highly that they rolled it up and took it along when they were forced to move to a new land.

Coaxing and charming groups into belief

There are several ways to provide a safe atmosphere where a leader can charm classes into belief. No one charms people into belief quite like Dorothy Heathcote. One of the secrets to her success lies in the carefully chosen first moments of the lesson. At the top of any lesson she looks the group over and thinks, "What will arrest their attention?" She looks for something to immediately hook the players into the problem that the lesson explores. Sometimes she uses an absurdity such as "Aren't you glad we took off our feet?" She may read a mysterious letter or tell the players that they are in danger. If players work with their own dreams, no matter how far fetched, they never have to be coaxed into belief.

A reluctant group might also be enticed through belief if the leader says something like, "and now through the magic of theatre, we will turn back the clock. . ." That form of statement puts the magic into the theatre rather than into the player's head. At other times a challenge may be appropriate. When working on a lesson based on Only One Woof, I said, "I just don't see how we can go on when there is no money for prizes." The eight and nine-year-olds immediately became involved, counting off many ways money could be earned for the prizes, and then they jumped into playing out some of the ways.

Cecily O'Neill has observed that children in thematic drama always begin in stereotype, but they drop it as belief grows. She often uses the players' own ideas and stories to charm them into belief. It is important for the leader to detect details which may be standing in the way of commitment. In the Potawatomi dramas, Meta did not like her assigned name, "Cousin Tweeter." After the tribe voted that she could change her name, she was much happier and participated wholeheartedly in the drama.

Visualizing in role

Imagination is improved through visualization. When a group of adults at a conference were put through Cecily O'Neill's lesson "The Haunted House," they discussed their commitment to the story and their belief. One of the things that they agreed upon was that once they could visualize the haunted house, they became much more deeply involved in their roles. In recent years there has been a great deal of research by drama specialists into the connection between imagination and imaging first brought to the attention of educators by Jean Piaget. Maxwell Maltz deals with this relationship in Psycho-Cybernetics. The American authority on this subject is Helene Rosenberg of Rutgers University. Her book, Creative Drama and Imagination: Transforming Ideas into Action, describes the method for her work and expands on the theory.

Leaders need to pay attention to visualization and belief. When belief starts to slip, they should concentrate on visualizing the imagined scene. Many drama leaders develop story telling skills which can help both performers and listeners visualize.

Put Your Mother on the Ceiling by Richard DeMille is devoted to developing creativity in imaging. The adults I have used it with find it very helpful, once they get past their initial reaction that its suggested activities are too childish and silly for them. Its disadvantage for self training is that it is almost impossible to do alone. Most people concentrate on the imagined pictures much better if they are not reading at the same time they are visualizing, but are being read to by another person.

When leading groups in improvisation, it is important not to be over explicit with directions, or the participants may fall into cliched behavior. Every player must be free to develop his own picture of what is going on in the drama, or belief is eroded. The technique is to start the imaging process in the individual without creating a uniform group image, except as is absolutely necessary.

Thinking in role

The mind as well as the senses must be trained to operate like the character to be played. This is easy for children, harder for adults. With a little practice, most people can develop this skill by applying what Stanislavski called the "magic if." In this process, the person developing the role concentrates on how the times and circumstances have influenced his value system, habits, likes and dislikes. The following exercise was created to provide practice in the magic if.

Using the "Magic If" on *Our Town* characters, males insert "George," and females insert "Emily" in the first blank of each question. Then they answer the questions.

1. If I were _____, when would I rise each day?
2. If I were _____, I would be (adjective) _____ when I got up in the morning.
3. If I were _____, I would day dream about _____.
4. If I were ____, my jobs would include _____.
5. If I were ____, I would try to ___ and ____ my family.
6. If I were ____, I would do the following to get my love's attention.:
7. If I were ___, I would have the following plans for my future.
8. If I were ____, I would trust ____.
9. If I were ____, I would think the following about my father:

The next step in getting comfortable with working in role is for the leader to pick a character much like herself to think about. This the very thing that leaders will be asking the players to do. It is the "what if" game, and involves posing "what if" to a number of situations. "What if I had been born in Africa?" "What would life been like if I had lived in my grandmother and grandfather's youthful times?" "What would my feelings have been if I had been the oldest (youngest) in my family?"

Let us assume that the leader has picked the second example, thinking about her grandmother as herself. She could consider the times and jot down some notes about events that Grandmother may have experienced. Here are some questions and ideas to get her going.

We can begin by considering Grandmother's day. What was her bedroom like? Did she have to sleep on the couch? Did she have to share with someone younger? Was she in charge of other people, getting them up and making them breakfast? Did she have the luxury of a private bath? Did she wash up in her bedroom? Was the water cold?

What were Grandmother's dreams and goals? Was she content with her lot? Did she see any changes that she could make? Did she work for others? Did she learn from seeing the people around her? Was she in love? What material possessions did she value the most?

What did Grandmother look like? Did she consider herself pretty? Was she vain? Was she a shy girl who never had a date? Was she a girl with wild ways? Did she drive a fast little car?

We may now go to the park and try to see the world through Grandmother's eyes. What does Grandmother see? Do the young mothers strolling their babies remind her of her desire to have a home and family? Do the flowers make her think about how her mother insists that she do yard work? Do the young men on the playing field see Grandmother? Does she see them?

Finally we may try out a performance of Grandmother for others. We tell our class that we are going to play Grandmother (or Mrs. Stone if we want to keep Grandmother's identity a secret). "I had some very interesting experiences in my youth, and I want to share them with you." Using the same technique, it is now possible to move on to a character in a great drama.

Belief and commitment is not only built before a lesson, but during a lesson as well. One of the things that helps people believe and want to go on in a lesson is the investment of time and work. Letter writing in character helps to build belief. One university student who wrote a letter in role commented, "That letter helped us to personally develop a character without fear of ridicule and with group restraints."

Choosing roles

In her work, Cecily O'Neill has researched how to use the layers of identity typical of the great dramas to deepen belief. Characters in plays often put on disguises and pretend to be someone else. Several layers of identity are a staple of most comedy, and much tragedy. One needs only to think of

Shakespeare's comedies to remember how he likes to take a young boy actor who is playing a girl in a play, and dress him up like and boy. This, of course, makes it much easier to believe when the girl walks like a boy, because "she" really is a he, and when a boy talks like a girl talking like a boy, because "she" really is a he. This idea is an extension of the notions of revealing and hiding identity.

To apply this notion of layers of belief to a play for young people, think about *The Ice Wolf*. In it an Eskimo girl who looks like a Caucasian becomes a wolf. Eventually the wolf becomes a spirit, freeing the girl inside. Under these stage roles there would also be the reality of the actress playing the girl/wolf/spirit.

O'Neill uses this technique when she arrives at the little pig's door to announce in a gruff voice that she is the postman and has a package for the class. The children have to figure out through questioning and discussion with each other if this is a nice woman, a wicked wolf, or a kindly postman. The problems posed by this layering of character deepens belief. Once accustomed to this convention, the players in the Potawatomi lessons had no trouble believing that Traveling Bluebird also was the Medicine Woman. Is this their teacher, or Bluebird, Medicine Woman, or The Great Kinnekinic with whom the children speak? When a group of seven year olds set up a display in the museum, were the children adult museum workers, the ancient Egyptians, or statues? Drama lessons will have greatly enriched belief if multi-layers of characterization are incorporated.

Suspension of disbelief is additionally strengthened as the players play the second and third layers of identity. It may be threatening to play the wolf in "Red Riding Hood," but it may be fun to play the wolf playing Grandmother; for the wolf may not be a very good actor, and the person in role doesn't have to be totally convincing as Grandmother.

Acting teacher Robert Cohen refers to layers of belief in *Acting Power*, demonstrating the fact that even a character who is not in disguise is rarely "playing it straight." He refers to the masks adults wear in public to cover their true emotions. Cohen calls this "playing the opposite." Examples abound. A man I know looked pleasant for three hours at a party the evening of the very day he had all of his lower teeth pulled! He was playing the opposite. When my students come into a class to take a test and smile at me with all the confidence in the world, they are playing the opposite. Even at the death of a loved one, we English speakers try to keep a stiff upper lip.

If an actress' role is Cinderella, she knows that she feels sad, but she must not mope about too much, for Cinderella surely does not want everyone to look directly into her heart of hearts. Even third graders know that polite society calls for true emotions to be masked. A number of times in the Potawatomi adventure after a highly emotional sequence, Meta came to me in confidence and told me that she was only kidding. To believe, there must be subtle layers of pretense as well as sincerity.

What if participants refuse to suspend disbelief?

It happens occasionally. What can a leader do in this case? In the Potawatomi drama, Nicole's insistence that I had to be Mrs. Allen, even after she killed me, is an example. I could not let Mrs. Allen come back because some of the sessions needed to center around working through her murder. Nicole insisted that I could not possibly be my other persona, Traveling Bluebird, although Traveling Bluebird had been carefully introduced the first day of the lessons. It was only because I kept repeating that I was Traveling Bluebird, and that I could bring proof that I was, that she let me go on with the work. Bringing the blue ceramic bird to the lesson the next day satisfied her "doubt." It allowed her to suspend disbelief.

Adult classes that I work with often will go along with mental and verbal play, but when I ask them to do something physical, they are very reluctant. This is particularly true of senior citizens. Even in the university class that worked on "Oregon or Bust!" half of the class resisted going "hunting for deer" while the other looked for the lost valuables in the river bed after a wagon tipped over. Yet when I asked the same group to pack their (imaginary) remaining possessions after the deer hunting, they were quite happy to do so. Adults will move much more slowly into physical commitment, and it will probably discourage them if the leader makes an issue of their reluctance.

A simple bit of action may help older players gain confidence. Asking the students to pose for a sculptor who was commemorating their crossing the mountains as they skinned the deer, might have been easier for them to do. In the first hour of a lesson about a mystery aboard a ship, senior citizen players were much happier letting their college class partners make tableaux than doing it themselves. But time and patience helped them commit physically and become comfortable with developing a character in action.

Sometimes players get the giggles, and then everyone loses concentration. When this happens, it is fine to let them giggle until they can giggle no more. After all, this is drama, not a formal production. Being human must be one of drama's most important traits, and breaking up is a very human thing to do. Nervousness, embarrassment, and reactions to strange situations may cause giggles. When leaders introduce new ideas to young people, they should expect them to giggle the first time around. Players eventually get past the giggles. Boredom is a great cure for the giggles and asking someone to giggle as long and hard as she can may be the ultimate cure.

Under other circumstances, it is all right to drop the drama lesson for the day and do something else. Some days I don't want to pretend, either. The leader can use the allotted time for research or another aspect of the work such as developing a sense of place rather than character. Being able to put down the mask is not a luxury a professional actor can afford. When I am in a formal play, I have to pretend, like it of not. But, thematic drama is not the professional theatre, and under most circumstances players' moods deserve some recognition and respect. Recognizing a group's mood may earn much appreciation, if not love. Leaders just shouldn't let the group think that they have given up on the project or "gone soft." They should make it clear that the group will have to return to the work in the next lesson and take comfort that research and developing a sense of place can be a step toward building belief itself.

If leaders find that they still have trouble believing and still have stage fright, they need to remember that this is normal. Actress Helen Hayes fought severe stage fright all of her life. No one would want teachers, politicians, or baseball players to be so relaxed about public performance that they did not do their best. More experience in public speaking, teaching, and public performance of all kinds will help put leaders more at ease. Concentrating on what is being said helps. A lot of stage fright seems to be the result of the speaker paying too much attention to how she is speaking and not enough to what she is saying, concentrating on whether the listener is getting the message and how she feels and what she thinks. Holding a prop in the hand and moving about naturally helps to burn up the excess adrenaline that is producing sweaty palms and shaking knees. Courses in speech and acting may provide the experience to put one at ease.

Understanding suspension of disbelief has its philosophical and complicated side, but in the end, the best advice for working in this basic aspect of drama is to have fun and play as in childhood.

Sources

ADLER, RONALD B. and NEIL TOWNE. *Looking Out, Looking In.* 5th Ed. New York: Holt, Rinehart and Winston, 1990.

COHEN, ROBERT. *Acting Power.* New York: Mayfield Publishing Company, 1978.

DEMILLE, RICHARD. *Put Your Mother on the Ceiling.* New York: The Viking Press, 1973.

FURTH, HANS. *Piaget for Teachers.* Englewood Cliffs N.J.: Prentice-Hall, 1970.

KASE-POLISINI, JUDITH. *The Creative Drama Book: Three Approaches.* New Orleans: The Anchorage Press, 1988.

KLIMO, JONATHAN. "The Lucid and the Ludic," *Drama as a Meaning Maker*, ed. Judith Kase-Polisini. University Press of America, 1989, pp. 133-148.

MAXWELL MALTZ, *Psycho-Cybernetics.* Englewood Cliffs, NJ: Prentice Hall, 1960.

O'NEILL, CECILY. "The Articles of Dramatic Action," *Drama Contact No. 13*, pp. 3-5.

ROSENBERG, HELENE. *Creative Drama and Imagination: Transforming Ideas into Action.* New York: Holt, Rinehart and Winston, 1987.

ROSS, RAYMOND S. *Speech Communications.* 8th Ed. New York: Mayfield Publishing Co., 1985.

SMITH, WALLACE. "Responses to What's Interesting in Children's Theatre." in *Children's Theatre: Creative Drama and Learning.* Ed. Judith Kase-Polisini. New York: University Press of America, 1984, p. 56.

QUESTIONING IN ROLE

*"Asking the right question is the teacher's
most important job."*

Dorothy Heathcote

This chapter presents

• *real and rhetorical questions;*

• *types of questions;*

• *and accepting answers.*

There can be no doubt that asking questions is the most important way to shape the drama. As common experiences build on tensions, questions move lessons to interesting situations. At the museum class exploring life in Michigan 150 years ago, the experience of all who had come to a sparsely inhabited land was being explored. The leader started the lesson with, "My, so many trees, and so tall. Everywhere you look. Magnificent and beautiful. What are we to do?" In the drama, "Passage on 'The Anne'" where the brotherhood of those who gave up everything to achieve freedom of worship was being explored, the lesson began with the distribution of letters from loved ones in the new world. The leader asked, "What is the word from our friends?" Immediately the players are into the thought and action of the drama.

Teachers' questions are often rhetorical and do not free the drama. In fact, they may suppress it. They pose questions which judge the learners or point out the teacher's knowledge while displaying the student's lack of knowledge. But the teacher knows the answer. In good drama questioning, the teacher is not asking rhetorical questions or questions which evaluate the learner. The teacher, rather, asks questions to keep the drama lively and exciting, and to move the participants to a deeper understanding of their emotions, their role in the dramatized society, and intellectual concepts inherent in the play. "Have you milked the cows?" "Do you trust the postman?" "Are you seasick?" "What will we do if the baby dies?"

Dennis Palmer Wolf of Project Zero point out that "School hallways are full of adolescents whose major mode of learning is to copy, examine or argue with the knowledge of their peers." Most teacher strategies do not take into account these natural modes of learning. Rarely do students question each other in the classroom, and teachers assume that students have little to teach them.

Questions free players and give them power. Only the players know the answers, and these answers have the power to change the direction of the story, making it the players' own. Those in such a drama soon realize that their answers matter and that they can influence the plot as well as other participants through their action and character. "If you make it through this, will you help your sister?" "When you give back the diamonds, will the others give up theirs?" Teaching in role gives the group the power of the playwright who makes artistic decisions. Players' answers determine what scenes will be played and how and where they will take place, and in what sequence they will occur. "Shall we have the next scene take place in the saloon or at the church?" "Should the bartender be in this scene?" "Will the ponies need a lot of care?"

Questions deepen the drama, moving it from shallow pantomime to serious thought and emotion. To a group of six-year-olds, chopping down trees, one may ask, "How do you keep from being hit by the falling trees?" To a group of nine-year-olds the leader may ask, "Will the community demand that Jason be punished?" or "Is there a way to make up for Anatou's death?" To a group of high school students following Gandhi to the sea, the leader asks, "Do you have the courage to be beaten when we defy the English law?" A group of Girl Scouts in a drama about a hike in the Alps, encountered injured people caught in a landslide. The leader asked, "Shall we continue our hike, or shall we see what can be done for these people?" To any player in a dangerous position the leaders might pose, "What is your deepest fear?"

The four functions of questions

1. The first is to **seek information**. With the information found, the leader and the group build the drama. Possible questions that seek information might be "What time are we to meet the witch?" "Have you found the treasure?" "What do you want to plant in the garden?" "Are you done planning the houses?" "Did you hear George and Emily at the soda fountain?"

    Questions that seek information may encourage the class to go to the library or to re-read assigned lessons. Questions may encourage them to do on-site research, to set up experiments or to ask questions of others. Questioning in this manner encourages students to develop the scientific attitude. Possible questions that could lead the students to deeper research might be, "Is there a way for us to find what herbs the Egyptians used in embalming?" "Are they available here, or do we have to trade for them?" "How many dark days can this plan survive?" "What will happen if we stop eating vegetables?" "Even if the ship leaks, can we make it to America?"

    The leader should not know all the answers to the questions they ask. If leaders know the answers readily, these questions may be rhetorical. Then the class will answer such questions because they are "good students," and the leader is a "good teacher." They know that the leader knows the answer, so there is really no good reason why they can't just ask that person to tell them the answer. In problem solving situations, however, there is no good reason to withhold information.

2. Questions also **give information**. Asking a question is an interesting and natural way for a leader to begin a drama or to move a story along when it may be getting a bit too static. The question, "What shall we

do about the children?" may be seeking information, but it may also be giving the information that the children need to fit into the plans. Information questions may also introduce a fact that needs to be considered. The question, "Do you think that your trunk might weigh over the 50 pound limit?" may give the information there is a limit to the amount of goods one may take over the mountains to Oregon. "Is this the fast-acting poison Romeo takes?" contains the information that Romeo takes poison. "Have you seen my Captain's hat?" offers the information that you may be a captain. By casting information in questions, participants have the exciting task of trying to make sense of bits of information in a life-like way. No one sits down and explains everything to anyone in life. Every day we have to put clues together to figure out who is related to whom, who has what job, who is loved by his spouse, who is just barely making it financially. Putting the clues together builds belief and interest in the drama, just it does in life. Often young people will reciprocate leader questions with questions containing additional clues. Then a true "play," develops, with clues bouncing back and forth among the players and the leaders, creating a framework upon which the drama may hang.

3.   Questions may also be used as a **technique** for control. By making slow and quiet movements, without the possibility of touching or giggling, many of the discipline problems in a theatre piece are solved. Slow, quiet seriousness can be introduced through questions as well as through other techniques. Heathcote asked of a group, "How can we make sure the king won't hear us?" Similar questions might be, "When we attack the Ice Wolf, how can we possibly not be seen or heard?" "Did you tell me that a deer can hear a human 50 yards away?" "Will the Nazis be more apt to notice us if we run?" "Is it true that the witch can't see creatures in slow motion?" Many times these questions cannot be planned ahead, but it might be helpful for a leader to think through some control questions that might be appropriate for a lesson's content.

4.   Finally, questions force participants to **make decisions and clarify values.** This type of question deals with problem solving and exploring meanings in drama. They put emphasis on the brotherhoods and values, taking players deeply into the the story. They may define a moment to set the group to wondering. "I wonder what big decisions those who went with Beowulf made?" "It would make me happy and excited to capture the Ice Wolf. How would it make you feel?" "Should Goldilocks be punished?" "Why can't you let those poor people alone?" "If there is moss on the space ship, what will that mean?" Decision questions may be used to develop a new scene. "I wonder if Juliet's parents talked over the problem of her fascination for that Montague boy?" "If the pirates attack, should we escape?" "Can we let these sick people just lie here?"

What about answers?

Answers lie in on the other side of the coin from the questions, and answers have their own rule: answers given by players in a drama lesson must be accepted. The leader must be prepared for any answer and be able to use that answer. In the lesson, "Passage on 'The Anne,'" I had to be ready for the group to decide several different ways — to go to the new world, to stay in Holland, or to return to England. Leaders must look upon student answers to provide exciting possibilities that the leader never could have imagined, ideas which open as many doors as they close. In the lesson on "The Anne," a decision to stay in Holland would have opened as many options to explore as it closed. Perhaps I would have had to develop a scene going back 20 years where the Puritans were being persecuted by the Church of England, or gone ahead and shown how the English children were becoming "Dutch." Perhaps I could have skipped ahead ten years to a time when life in Plymouth Colony was more secure. There were any number of ways to go; but the "rule" of drama in role required that I use the children's decision. To contradict the player would be to break the code of honor in the game of pretend. If the drama teacher starts to accept some suggestions and reject others, the trust between leader and participant will be gone, and the drama will be dead. This is the challenge and excitement of improvisation.

Players' responses to questions need to be respected. When, in answer to a question, a participant tells a leader something silly or false or startling, he will have to accept that. If a leader asks a group of teenagers why someone is not participating, to egg him on, the teen may say that he is on drugs, the leader must seriously consider how to deal with this subject. It may be a cry for help, for it is a major concern of many young people; and it is only fair to give it a hearing. On the other hand, this could have been said just to get a response from the teacher. In that case, it can be disposed of rapidly. If the leader thinks that the group should spend some time dealing with the problem of drugs instead of the "planned lesson," he might avoid the silly aspects by distancing the subject. Perhaps the time could move ahead 25 years, and the youths are the teenage children of parents who developed their habits this year. A scene could be developed where a girl is ashamed to invite her friends home because of her father's addiction.

If a player says that a wild animal is tame or a tame animal is wild, the leader in role has to use that "fact" in the drama somehow. If the leader is told that Lowell is only an hour's canoe travel from Grand Rapids, he has to use this information. If the group decides that they want to go to war instead of make a treaty, the leader has to use that decision.

When the leader gets stumped

We all draw a blank occasionally. It is perfectly acceptable to call a recess of the drama to provide the leader and group some time to think about how to use a difficult suggestion. Only if the group makes a consensus agreement is it fair to drop a player's idea. The supportive climate may not be abandoned.

Although a supportive climate has been referred to earlier in this book, it has not been discussed fully. Jack R. Gibb's characteristics of supportive and defensive communication climates relate strongly to questioning. It has been found that education as well as communications is facilitated in the supportive climate. Gibb developed the following chart to contrast the two climates he identified. The chart can guide the establishment of a positive atmosphere in the drama room, one where questions can be attended to because students do not feel threatened.

THE GIBB CATEGORIES OF DEFENSIVE AND SUPPORTIVE BEHAVIORS

DEFENSIVE	SUPPORTIVE
1. evaluation	1. description
2. control	2. problem orientation
3. strategy	3. spontaneity
4. neutrality	4. empathy
5. superiority	5. equality
6. certainty	6. provisionalism

A glance at the list shows that thematic drama as it has been defined here exemplifies most of the supportive behaviors. It tends to not evaluate ideas and people. Drama is problem-oriented and spontaneous. Empathy and equality are major characteristics. Although certainty may come up in the drama on occasion, there is much more provisionalism than certainty. If the drama climate begins to have too many of the characteristics from the left hand column, the creative aspects of drama will be destroyed. Through intelligent and sensitive questioning, most of the supportive behaviors can prevail.

Dorothy Heathcote is right when she says that asking the right question is the teacher's most important job. Honest questions keep the players thinking, actively engaged in the drama and maintaining belief. If leaders learn how to ask good questions and to respond to players' answers in honest and exciting ways, they will be well on the way to developing successful dramas.

Sources

GIBB, JACK R. "Defensive Communication." *Journal of Communications.* 2 (September), 1961, pp. 141 through 148.

MORGAN, NORAH and JULIANA SAXTON. *Teaching Drama: A Mind of Many Wonders.* London: Hutchinson, 1987.

WOLF, DENNIS P. "Dramatic Imaginations." *Creative Drama in a Developmental Context.* Ed. Judith Kast-Polisini. New York: University Press of America, 1985, p. 316.

UNDERSTANDING ABILITY, INTEREST AND AGE

"There must be sensitivity to the class."
Cecily O'Neill

This chapter introduces aspects of child development in relation to thematic drama —

• *Physical and social*
• *Artistic*
• *Intellectual*
• *Moral*

CAN A CLASS OF FIFTH GRADERS BECOME ABSORBED IN A DRAMA LESSON based on a presidential campaign? Will a lesson on the life of Harriet Taubman or one on the life of Run DMC be approached more seriously by junior high school students? Will eight year olds be interested in developing a new breakfast cereal? These questions about age level appropriateness are typical ones the drama leader has to ask himself before he picks a topic to explore. And it is not easy. Boys cannot always be counted on to like the same activities as girls. Likely this is the most difficult part of the work in drama for the beginning leader. Even classroom teachers make mistakes in this area. While beginning leaders are just learning to understand young people's interests, seasoned teachers often doubt that their students will want to solve serious problems in pretend situations.

In answer to the questions above, the fifth graders did become very interested in the presidential campaign, because in role the students became advisors to the candidates, in some cases successful politicians who were the parents of the candidates. The junior high school students were so flattered to have an adult take a serious interest in one of their pop heroes that they were willing to work deeply in discovering the talents a rock star needs, the social alienation he must cope with, and the pressures of moving from poverty to wealth. When teachers helped another group of students, they "chose" the life of Harriet Taubman to play. That group went through the motions of the drama with less seriousness and intensity than the "Run DMC" group.

As for the cereal workship, the eight year old girls became very involved in naming the new cereal, creating television advertisements and designing attractive boxes, while the boys in the class only wanted to go on strike.

Developmental factors that impact the drama

Fortunately there are many good books to help us understand children as they grow. Project Zero, under the direction of Howard Gardner at Harvard University, has looked at the notion of talent and creativity. These researchers conclude that all children benefit from an arts education and that all children have talent that can be nurtured. Those with special gifts benefit from challenges, support, and knowledge that the struggle to be an artist is worthwhile.

Young children, they found, exhibit an enormous amount of creativity. They love to sing, draw, play-act. Then comes the point, at about age seven, when the child began to develop a sensitivity to the world around him. Child drama leader Peter Slade called this, "The Dawn of Seriousness." Dramas at this point become self-conscious and lose the fantasy quality of younger work. Within the framework of the drama children at this point are ready to move out of their personal concerns and deal with the problems of the world in the dramatic framework.

About mid-elementary age, this growing self awareness causes a crisis in creativity. This is a literal age and an age when students do not want to be different. Although very young people draw green skies, very few in junior high school draw green skies. If they draw something at that age, it must be as exact in color and proportion as can be.

The pre-adolescent looks at his drawing, writing, singing and acting and says "I am no good. People laugh at me when I create something. I am not as good as grown-ups. I cannot do this perfectly." Somewhere between fifth and eighth grades, many people put their artistic creativity in the closet. The same applies for drama. A partial cure for the problem of this age seems to be to pour on more artistic technique. In theatre this would include voice, movement, and interpretation skills.

In terms of gender, research is becoming more sophisticated and also helps us understand children's stages. Although there are few hard and fast conclusions that can be drawn at this time, we do know that by four or five years of age children have embraced gender stereotypes. Girls play with dolls. Boys play with pistols. Boys seem to become more aggressive as they grow older and little girls become more nurturing. Girls excel in nonverbal communication, and that may give them the edge in human interaction. Although differences between linguistic and math skills in the sexes seem to be getting less, once children identify with their own genders, differences do not disappear easily.

Where does theatre literacy begin and how does it grow?

In a 1993 research by the American Alliance for Theatre and Education's on theatre literacy, I surveyed current research in social "pretend" play relating it to theatre education. The findings have implications for all theatre teachers. Theatre literacy precedes other literacies and is the chosen medium for exploring the nature and purpose of the world.

Preschool

Preschool children are motivated more to participate in theatre when they contribute to the development of the plot, dialogue and other aspects of their play. At four and five children are able to cooperate to create theatre when they are in charge. They develop sequential scenes and understand cause and effect and the turn taking that dialogue requires. Preschoolers seem to prefer character and emotion over action.

Peer acceptance is the reward for theatre literacy in preschool. Through theatre preschoolers develop humor and clowning. By five they are proficient at characterization and mime. Pleasure is a central theme of social pretend play and grows out of peek-a-boo and other surprise games. Friendships and socialization are a major aspect of social pretend play.

Preschoolers have interest in the visual aspects of the theatre, including props, costumes and setting. They develop skills in directing, communicating to each other how to improve their work. In planning work for preschoolers, the leader should give the players adequate time. The children enjoy the planning part of the drama, and for it to be satisfactory, they must have enough time to do it their way.

Vivian Paley, one of the most innovative and thoughtful teachers of kindergartners, challenges the way we have thought about this age group. She uses the children's own stories to help come to terms with who they are. She had dreaded the boy's play, calling it rough and violent. On closer examination she found that the boy's play centered around right and wrong. Hidden behind the bravado of hitting each other, boys were working out how to have a just world. Of course Paley did not agree with the way that the boys achieved these ends, but she saw what was happening.

Paley believes that children's belief in magic is based on the knowledge that they will change into something else in the future —adults. For kindergartners, a person in character signals that some action will follow: the plumber arrives, there is a sink stopped up. Leadership goes to the children who understands the power of symbol. Judy is "mother" because she has the silver shoes. Teddy, a boy often on the outside, can achieve respect through storytelling because he can tell someone he will grow up to be Luke Skywalker, and his dream will be accepted.

Paley modeled bad behavior through imitation of the children's actions. The class thought it very funny, saying, "You did that part just right." She told a story about a boy named Franklin who was good and generous and understanding. In the classroom Franklin, who had formerly been disruptive, began to behave perfectly and proudly, just like the hero in the story. Paley tells us that the difference between telling someone that he is wrong and saying, "Pretend you are a boy who knows how to share," is that it tells the child he was wrong, and it also suggests heroic possibilities.

Girls' ideas of conflict proved to be very different from boys' conflict. Girls, Paley discovered, worry about unfair sharing practices. No bad guys, they said, can enter the play. Forceful entry must not be allowed. The boys, therefore, were not allowed to enter the doll corner, because the stories created by the two sexes do not mesh.

Early elementary grades

Children arrive at first grade with competency for constructing theatre, creating dramatic symbols based on transformations of objects, role, situation,and action. They can organize these symbols into dramatic episodes. They arrive at first grade as sophisticated players. They deserve to be respected as such. Observation of children as they approach early elementary school indicates that they depend less on theatre to understand their world, and interest wanes. What has not been explored is how to make theatre more interesting and challenging for six year olds than it has been in their past.

The cognitive development of six, seven and eight year olds deserves our attention. The child begins to make distinctions between the physical world and the psychological and intellectual world. Cause and effect (plot) in a drama can be discussed. Not all children, however, will be able to accept the reasons for a happening that the leader finds to be very clear. In the lesson "Prison at the River's Bend," children were uninterested in how the robber went from arrest to jail. Using the same story for junior high school students, the justice process might be the most interesting aspect.

Children do not generalize at this early age, accepting each example as a separate entity. It is very difficult for them to move from a specific case played out in a drama to a general law. Children this age love to classify, group and develop ascending and descending orders. Time becomes a part of their understanding. They know their own culture well and enjoy segmenting in their dramas. Collections can be a part of the drama as well as drawing and writing on the blackboard and in journals and notebooks. In "The Potawatomis" the children took great pleasure from making an extensive list of things to be put in a garden and in collecting objects for wampum necklaces.

Language becomes more sophisticated. Words can be used for power. Early elementary students are willing to answer questions and join in on round-robin stories. In "The Potawatomis" children wanted to become tribal storytellers; but they often were stumped as to what to say. In the question and answer time with the bird puppet, the players responded with language that reflected an emerging understanding of levels of formality. They found power in the dance chant, "Be Merciful to me, We want to live." Children are learning to use controls and to follow leaders.

Concentration is developing and children can play for two hours or more. Although a concept of death is forming, it was difficult for the children to accept Mrs. Allen's death, and refusing to take credit for it. By not coming back as Mrs. Allen, I attempted to help students deal with cause and effect.

In spatial intelligence, drawings show intellectual realism x-ray views, enlarged details, bird's-eye views. Children enjoy transforming spaces and are willing to imagine rivers, canoes, and maps, although they can not use the imagined objects as well as they will later.

Emotionally, children tend to live an extremes—totally happy or totally miserable. This is both a trial and a joy in drama class. Children show empathy to others. Although there seemed to be a certain cruelty in "Prison at the River's Bend," the children's better nature was found when the prisoners asked for their mothers. In fact, the young players expressed deep sympathy. Humor is visual and physical. Language jokes are beginning to be understood. Fears tie to separation, but a bit of fear can be entertaining. Companionship is sought with the same sex. Children enjoy a touch of magic, as with the bluebird figure and puppet in "The Potawatomis." The child thinks of himself as a misfit in his own family, hence the popularity of false mother stories. Moving to new families tests children's "true membership."

By the first grade, children know the basic moral laws and think that they are fixed and eternal. Wrong and right are usually very clear cut, although some ambiguity may enter. Children feel a strong code of obligation to friends, and the fairness of punishment becomes important. Since right and wrong are engrained so deeply engrained in the child's belief system, to go against them in the drama begs for trouble. The punishment Mrs. Allen got in "The Potawatomis" was just for this age. Although Mrs. Allen's plight of having to adhere to her husband's decisions did present a moral dilemma the children could understand, it was Mrs. Allen —the bearer of the bad news — with whom they could not sympathize.

Upper elementary

Nine, ten, eleven and twelve year olds continue to change and develop. They move beyond "why" questions about adhering to rules, and begin to understand mechanical functions, life phenomena, and spatial contacts. Some preteens even understand psychological motivation and logical explanation. In a drama about Odysseus children enjoyed wondering about Odysseus' motivations, and responding to the unknown. The players in "The Kish," however, had little interest in looking deeply into cause and effect.

Children this age can move into formal operations, developing hypotheses and testing them. They reason in propositions and argue by implication. Arguments become an important part of the drama. In "Election 1988," students gave good reasons for their choices as parents and as voter.

Mechanical relationships, model building and intellectual problems provide interesting challenges. Rostrum blocks and more props can be handled without distraction. The serious study of music begins. Musical backgrounds can be added. Scenes can be repeated and polished somewhat. Interest in classification continues. Players think through difficult and complex ideas such as

"Parents—Good or Bad?" They can respond to them with tableaux and art projects.

The nine year old knows that death will occur to him and all living things. Dramas that include the threat of death are meaningful and deeply felt. Players know that they are in the presence of other living actors, and that this moment will not return. The moment takes on new meaning.

Players now visualize physical relationships that are not tangible or familiar. Art shows more detail, with objects shown in relationships. Maps, drawings, costumes and masks become a part of the drama.

Young people this age develop strong attachments to same sex friends, cliques, and gangs, although there is rarely close physical "touching between sexes."

Players love adventure. They are become increasingly independent and enjoy vicarious excitement in sports, arts, and reading. They understand exciting plots, far away lands and times. "Election 1988" worked as a drama because it was about being rich and powerful, as well as being in the player's future. The strange and fearful hold fascination. Angry outbursts and withdrawal may occur. Ghost stories, tales and mysteries fascinate. Although there is not as much belief in magic as at an earlier age, there is a longing for magic, and its introduction is acceptable if prefaced with thinking about how wonderful it would be.

Players take great pleasure in personal achievement. They can take the cloak of heroism and problem-solve in a safe environment. Players sympathize with pain, sorrow, fear, joy and love. Although they may seem very blase, they are easily aroused to sympathy during the drama. Humor continues to be visual and physical. But riddles and stories which show superiority begin to enter in. Story telling and gibberish are popular.

In the moral and ethical arena, there is still the operation by rules and a fear of guilt. Dramas about adherence to rules are interesting. Groups enjoy meting out simple justice as in "The Land of the Kish." Although they may not comprehend degrees of rightness and wrongness, this age group knows that others may not see a situation from their point of view. Justice is based on reciprocity, although there may be some identification with the punished player. Knowledge that justice is not always served in life grows with the players. Students spend a great deal of time working out "fair" solutions. They may demand that endings reward heroes and that villains be made to pay for their crimes. The most important moral obligation is to friends, not adults. Rules may be changed if there is agreement. Players at this age are able to foresee outcomes and know that doing harmful acts may cause censure. This quality in nine through twelve year olds makes adventures such as "Odysseus" interesting because players can see the possible trouble Odysseus may encounter.

Young teens

The thirteen, fourteen and fifteen year olds exhibit other traits. As to their cognition, they can test hypothesis, argue from propositions, and pick out errors in reasoning. Players try several endings and discuss the validity of each. Mental capacities grow at this period, as the world opens to the teen.

Players open their minds to new ideas and like to be given intellectual challenges that move them out into the great world where no problem is too big. It does not seem too great a leap to move from Muskegon, Michigan to the glamorous world of a rap star. It is not too great to imagine oneself moving across India with Gandhi, bringing the British to the negotiation table through nonviolence.

In the spatial realm players enjoy both examining details and the larger picture, as they did in segmenting "Run DMC," and making the final choices for enactment. Players understand mechanical/spatial interactions. There is much attention to detail in dress and self presentation. Settings now become important to players, and where the scene takes place can become a part of cause and effect. How the bus was set up in "The Rosa Parks Story" was very important to junior high school players, and they worked long and hard developing where Rosa would be seated, how the bus driver's attention would be pointed, and where and how whites and African-Americans pointed their fingers and held their bodies.

Feelings are intense and extreme at this age. Players know about private suffering. They imagine impossible romances, and crushes are common. Mood swings may make players difficult to work with, yet a player's mood may provide a starting point. Since Ulysses, for example, has such extreme moods, one way to make "The Odyssey" lesson appropriate for young teens would be to use the emotional hostility so often found in teenagers as a beginning for working on that story.

Players have a hard time controlling giggles. As with all things in the drama, one should not despair but put the quality to use. The giggles could become an important part of a scene as they did in "Run DMC" in a concert.

Physical changes cause awkwardness which in turn cause feelings of difference and unacceptance. Girls are ready for heterosexual social occasions, while boys may not be. Players of this age are ready to work with the opposite sex, if not ready to date them. They may even delight in playing scenes with sexual overtones, as in one where "Run's" fans tore off his shirt.

The desire for peer approval makes work in groups unusually dynamic. A predilection to agreement helps scene development. Teens emulate the behavior of the person they most admire. This is an ideal time to work on projects based on the lives of great heroes.

In contrast, this is the age of rebellion and yearning for independence. Adult-imposed rules are to be broken. Heros like Rosa Parks and Gandhi, who broke the rules for a higher purpose, provide role models which are positive, yet feed on the desire for rebellious behavior.

Youth are more aware of all kinds of jokes, double meaning, and sex as a basis of jokes. Outsiders are to be ridiculed. Care must be taken to use these characteristics for positive action in the drama lesson. Dramas that encourage acceptance may help players become more sensitive. In the drama "Run DMC," players were able to see themselves as grown up and able to move in adult society gracefully and with authority.

Most players of this age respond to a level of conformity. Some obey rules to satisfy individual conscience. Endings usually have to conform to rules, but rules may be changed through the democratic process. Players enjoy working out elaborate societies with new rules that they can test. Justice and fairness is a strong feeling at this stage. Players know that wickedness may go unpunished if one is not caught. Forgiveness and mitigation of punishments are accepted by those over thirteen.

The above, then, are some of the characteristics of young people at four distinct stages. They are general guidelines. Every large group has some children with younger characteristics and some in more advanced stages. Learning the ages levels comes with practice, but these examples may help in planning those first difficult meetings with a new group.

Sources

DAVIS, JED H. and MARY JANE WATKINS EVANS. Theatre, Children and Youth. New Orleans: Anchorage Press, 1982.

DEMILLE, RICHARD. *Put Your Mother on the Ceiling.* New York: The Viking Press, 1973.

PALEY, VIVIAN Gussin. Boys and Girls: Superheroes in the Doll Corner. Chicago: University of Chicago Press, 1984.

_____ . Wally's Stories. Cambridge, MA.: Harvard University Press, 1981.

SHAPIRO, LAURA. "Guns and Dolls," *Newsweek,* May 28, 1990, pp. 56-65.

WORKING WITH A PARTNER

"Live while ye may,
Yet happy pair."

John Milton

This chapter shows how partners

• *reflect society and theatre;*

• *help and support each other;*

• *and affect drama structure.*

THE MAJORITY OF UNIVERSITY STUDENTS WHO TOOK DRAMA CLASSES, research has shown, did not teach drama when they got to the classroom. We do not know why, but it may be that it is too much of a risk and takes great effort. School administrators do not support teachers in developing programs and learning as they make mistakes. To combat these problems, partner work in thematic drama encourages beginners and supports experienced teachers. It seems a solution to the anxiety and loneliness of drama work in the classroom.

Working in partnership eases the amount of responsibility and work while providing more dramatic possibilities. Two people encourage, complement, and critique each other. They allow the drama to have lower and higher ranked leader roles simultaneously, and provide dramas with both a protagonist and antagonist. Working in teams is appropriate to the art of theatre. Theatre art is always a group art, exploring the social aspects of the tribe and the city state. Theatre is based in cooperation among actors, the playwright, the director, designers, musicians and box office staff. Further, a successful theatrical event results from cooperation between performers and the audience. Partnerships model cooperation and discourage the development of individual "stars" and undesirable "artistic temperament."

In America, team work is an important common value. We see it in sports, youth clubs, and music activities as well as the workplace. Sociologists tell us that it is groups working cooperatively who will solve the problems of the world, no lone heroes. We need only to look at the almost bloodless revolution against Communism of the early 1990's to see how groups of people are the real heroes of history. Partnering models this kind of problem solving.

Partners offer advantages in an institutional structure.

Administrators tend to look more favorably upon projects planned and executed by more than one teacher in the school. Other teachers will be more accepting if they see that thematic drama is something in which a large part of the school can participate. Partnerships work. In some schools, whole buildings have chosen a theme to explore through drama for an entire school year, with all of the staff working together in different combinations on different days.

Partnering often helps to solve problems of the leader in role

One can play a powerful person while the other plays what Heathcote calls an "I don't know role." In "The Land of the Kish," the college students played lowly slaves, women the Kish had captured in war. The sixth grade teacher was their defeated queen. I played the middle level role of the Old Princess of the Kish. In the lesson "Passage on the Anne," the classroom teacher, Russell Keil, played a powerful character unscrupulously trying to get the Pilgrim's money, while I played a high-principled, rather indecisive woman trying to carry out her son's wishes.

In the Potawatomi lessons, Princess Sunflower played a very high status role, while Mrs. Allen proved totally helpless. Traveling Bluebird was not especially powerful, except in her magical trances. When Traveling Bluebird went into a trance, the Princess was able to protect the players from harm and encourage them to deepen the work. My role as Senator Gardner, who appeared on the final day of the workshop, was very powerful, while the princess grew weaker in the company of the whites.

At the Grand Rapids Public Museum six and seven year olds had the powerful role of Michigan pioneers, people able to decisively bring civilization to a wilderness. The leader played their weak old grandmother, while college students played non-English speaking immigrants who had lost their husbands in a shipwreck on Lake Michigan. In each of these instances, the various roles complemented each other. Without two or more leaders to play these roles, there could not have been this great a variety in characterization in the extended lesson.

Partnering facilities the application of classic dramatic structures to thematic drama

It allows for one partner to play the antagonist and another to play the leader of the group of protagonists. One leader may encourage plot development while the other deepens thought; thus more versatility in dramatic action is possible with two or more adult drama leaders, and two leaders make it possible to have more surprise within the story. In the Potawatomi drama, I could lead the group while my partner set up the naming ceremony. She could lead the group in a discussion while I donned the Medicine Woman costume.

There are personal advantages to working with a partner

Sometimes a leader may feel that she is too tired, too sick, too discouraged to go on with a drama lesson. The fact that there is someone depending on the leader may help her continue in her work. When a lesson is going properly, the partner can assure the other that the work is all right. Drama is not about success, but about process. A partner can help to show the other where she has succeeded even when she is not seeing success in her work. And very importantly, partners can step in when the other needs help in disciplining the group.

A partners can help another see her weaknesses. She can fill in for a partner who may lack a skill or talent. One may be better at the language aspects of the lesson, gibberish and high level speech, while the other is good at calming the group after it has had a lively time in some activity. In the Potawatomi sessions, Princess Sunflower's ability to lead quietly, often in a befuddled manner, was balanced by Traveling Bluebird's use of puppetry.

Scheduling

Within a school, two leaders working together will mean adjusting schedules. Perhaps the teachers' classes can meet to work together. This could make a very large and perhaps unmanageable class, but other configurations are possible. There are way to schedule A and B teachers so that both can work in A's class one time and B's the next. Possible solutions could be to work during a gym class, to rotate recesses or lunches, or to leave one class with a teacher's aide or the principal herself. The same considerations have to be made in theatre and recreational settings. Partnering need not double the budget or the amount of work.

The partner need not be a colleague at the same institution. Working thematically is as exciting for a leader as it is for the players. Many people who love acting appreciate the experiences and freedom that thematic drama work gives them. A teacher may ask a volunteer; partners may be found at a community theatre, where there will be many people who are involved in the theatre because they love the art. Because parents are so interested in their children's growth in the arts, they make good leaders. Parents with interest in theatre, or the subject matter of the thematic work, may enjoy and excel in the work. Many classes have a teacher's aid who may make a good partner. A brother, sister, child, spouse, or neighbor may be a partner.

Professional actors, ex-actors and potential actors all are possible partners.

Detroit's Attic Theatre and The Detroit Public Schools have been working together to bring thematic drama experiences into the classrooms of elementary, junior high and senior high schools for several years. In this project teachers paired with professional actors. In the beginning teachers were excited about the possibilities of the experience, whereas the actors were more reluctant. But by the end of the eighth week of the residency, the actors and teachers were totally convinced that this is an excellent way to bring new ideas and techniques into classes. The actors were amazed and delighted with this way of using their talents in a new field of creativity. They immediately began to use the techniques with additional groups. The Artistic Director of the theatre became so enthusiastic about thematic work that she used some drama in role at a board meeting.

Partnerships are open to the problems of any relationship. One problem that can develop is an adult-dominated drama. The two leaders must be careful to let the problem solving be done by the players. They must both be engaged deeply in the players' interests and have great enthusiasm for and love of the theatre. When working with a partner, it is important to be sensitive to her point of view and to keep feelings and information checked through communication. When a leader asks someone to work on a session, she needs to leave herself a way out. It may help for partners to think of themselves in a free lance arrangement, rather than a full time partnership.

Often in my personal work I take a student for a partner because of the difficulty of scheduling work with peers, and the lack of peers in my community. Although this usually works out well, at times it is not ideal. A peer relationship would help my work, for a peer is more free to offer suggestions, more equally grounded in theory and experience, and more willing to make judgements about outcomes.

In looking for a partner, there are several characteristics that need checking. Communication research seems to show that we do best in relationships with people who are basically like us, but different enough to bring new ideas to the relationship. Two characteristics to be noted are a sense of humor and a compatible philosophy of educational theatre. Here is a list of aspects to consider.

1. How does she use her time? Will she work at a compatible pace? What are her ideas about time in the drama lesson itself?

2. How flexible is she? If something goes awry, can she improvise? Does she enjoy improvisation? Can she change a lesson mid-stream? Can she be both a leader and follower? Can she give power to the players?

3. Will she enjoy taking risks?

4. What is her planning style? Is it flexible? Will she be willing to let the other do her share of the planning?

5. What is her area of expertise? Is she willing to share it? Is she interested in going to the library to research what she doesn't know? Does she like to learn new things?

6. Who is she? What are her values? Will she complement the other when teaching brotherhoods?

7. What is her interest in detail? Is she a stickler for details? Do the two leaders balance each other in this area?

8. Is she genuinely interested in drama? What is her attention span for projects?

9. What is her discipline style? Can she tolerate the amount of freedom of movement and speech which drama requires?

10. Does she communicate openly? Can the leaders be frank with each other? Can they tell each other if something is not going well? Can they give each other compliments?

11. Does she have a good sense of humor? Can she laugh at herself?

Working with various partners can be one of the most rewarding aspects of teaching drama. It supports all goals of drama work: drama/theatre, content, and group cooperation.

Sources

KARDASH, ANNE M. and LIN WRIGHT. "Does Creative Drama Benefit Elementary School Students; a Meta-Analysis." *Youth Theatre Journal.* 1:3, pp. 11 through 18.

TEACHING VALUES IN ROLE

"Entertainment is an expression of our nature — the creature who asks where and how and why and whither."

Robert Coles

This chapter introduces

• *formal studies of American values;*

• *ways to study self values;*

• *the relationship of violence and conflict to drama lessons;*

• *and what drama teachers can do.*

THE DRAMA LEADER MUST TEACH WHAT HE KNOWS, AND ALSO WHO HE IS. Teaching in role puts the leader in positions where he must make ethical and moral decisions on the spot. Loved and respected artists are keenly aware of the values they hope to pass on to their public. Paul Robeson, the great American opera singer and actor, always worked from his values. If his value were compromised he did not work. On his tombstone are his words, "The artist must make up his mind to be free or slave." That might well be the motto of the teacher of thematic drama.

Teaching thematically means getting in touch with values, those of North Americans in general, your own, and those of your students. Two landmark studies of United States citizens' values were made by Edward D. Steele and Charles W. Redding. The following are seventeen values they uncovered, appearing in descending order:

1. Puritan and pioneer morality
2. The individual
3. Achievement and sucess
4. Change is progress
5. Ethical equality
6. Equality of opportunity
7. Effort and optimism
8. Efficiency, practicality and pragmatism
9. Rejection of authority
10. Science and secular rationalism
11. Sociability
12. Material comfort
13. Quantification
14. External conformity
15. Humor
16. Generosity and consideration
17. Patriotism

A Harris poll showed the following values of American males. They, too, are listed in descending order.

1. Health
2. Love
3. Peace of mind
4. Family life
5. Work
6. Friends
7. Respect from others
8. Education
9. Religion
10. Money

Many thinkers worry that the values and ethics of Americans are eroding. Some writers even declare that ethics are at an all-time low. The motivations of the participants in the Iran-Contra scandal; clergymen found padding their pockets handsomely with the hard-earned contributions of those on fixed income; and Wall Street scandals illustrate the point. Bernice Kanner says that although it is very chic for companies to offer ethics seminars, they are usually only taught to top management. Values need to be taught to all Americans, not just a few. Kranner quotes New York Councilwoman Ruth Messinger who believes that greed has become a totally legitimate force in the workplace. Workers go into enterprises to see what they can get out of the companies, and they whitewash everything that could be labeled wrong.

How Americans lost their sense of the old values is still a topic of debate. Some people believe that it is a decline in religion which caused this. Harvey Cox of Harvard Divinity School blames the erosions of morals in part on the compromise made between politics and religion at the turn of the century. At that time "The state [promised that it] would not interfere in matters of heaven or the soul. In return, religion would keep its nose out of 'the world.'" (*Religion in the Secular City*, Simon & Schuster, 1984.)

Others believe that the mobile society that Americans live in has made community impossible. One urban church did not find it possible to define the "community" that it should serve. As another cause, Kanner believes that most Americans have difficulty with expectations. We have come to expect wealth from life, and since we feel that we deserve material wealth, we go for it in any way that we possibly can. There are other people who will point their fingers at television, at young people, at depersonalization in the work place, at the new morality, at yuppies. No matter what the cause, however, there is a great need for those who work with young people to teach who they are.

How values develop

Values develop over a long period of time, through the experiences of valued others and exposure to life and books. Louis Kolberg's, Carol Gilligan's, and Robert Coles' studies indicate that people's values develop throughout life. Although it is helpful to become familiar with the studies of values held by North Americans, these studies may not provide a deep enough look into our individual selves. One reason we may have trouble finding our own values is that talking about them is not done much in polite company in the United States. Dorothy Heathcote has commented that her inspiration for work with children comes from books on the human condition. Others may find inspiration through nature, practicing a formal religion, or volunteer work. It is helpful to probe for values exposed in one's childhood. Thinking about some favorite childhood stories is one interesting exercise to start remembering the development of values. In this exercise one names a childhood story and the character with whom he identified. He examines the other characters and how they are similar to his life, then asks if this story relates to his life now. Has the story become a self-fulfilling prophecy? What values did the story put forth, and how are they similar to the values held now?

It may help a drama leader to get in touch with values by talking to friends and students, to tell each other stories and discuss experiences, daydreams and the dreams you dream at night.

Exercises to bring forth values

Another values clarification exercise comes from Cecily O'Neill. The leader places players in the role of fairy godparents who present "gifts" to a baby. A bundle is passed around the group and each member bestows personality characteristics as a gift to this new child. This technique is used in the lessons "Run DMC" and "The House of Christine." Another exercise centered on values is one which explores building a memorial to an idea or person. In the lesson "Honoring Charlotte," players were challenged to plan a celebration of their famous ancestor, Charlotte. One group who played this lesson planned a spelling contest, a twisters contest, and an heroic statue. The lesson "Indian Salt Belongs to India" has a memorial as a component. Such lessons provide excellent reflection on the themes and values encountered in life and fiction.

Dorothy Heathcote's favorite situation for examining values involves what she calls the "Treasure Burden." With every treasure, she says, comes a burden, and the weight of the burden as well as the joy of the treasure must be explored in a drama. "With the blessing comes the curse. Either take it all or take nothing." An example of the treasure burden is found in "Run DMC" where the players discovered that in some ways public life destroys private life. In their work, Run found himself unable to walk down the street without having strangers touch him, and old friends, relatives, and even strangers beg him for money.

Drama teachers who work in church schools, theatres and in other institutions may have some very clear values to teach. In church school teaching, values must be a part of the lesson. In theatre programs and recreation departments there is less concern over the separation of church and state than in the public schools, so community values may be more freely discussed. The United Kingdom mandates that Christian values be taught in the schools. Therefore lessons that Heathcote may have felt compelled to teach, present subject matter that would be impossible for Americans to use in the schools.

With religion a taboo subject (and that must be clear in the drama leader's mind), what values can be taught in America's public schools?

Fortunately, researchers have described an American system of values listed earlier, and these should be acceptable to teach in any setting. They provide a starting point. A leader may teach within the framework of the values that Americans hold in common — that is our freedom of speech. There is a need for all teachers to teach integrity and love and support in their classrooms, and these are not the property of any one religion, but the values of good people everywhere.

Whatever the circumstance, it will be helpful to review the techniques for deepening values within drama experiences.

- Stop to reflect
- Slow the pace of the drama
- Impose rituals
- Classify responses
- Interject probes
- Integrate additional art forms
- Use symbols

Dealing with violence

Any exploration of values in the classroom in the United States tody must deal with the preoccupation Americans have with violence. This preoccupation has become a special interest of mine. How can it help but be when as I write this, a high-school student in a nearby city shot another student, and one of my theatre advisees was murdered in June. Americans have a tremendous appetite for violence. The game of teacher versus student that often dominates the classroom may be in some instances only a microcosm of the hostility seen in the bigger world.

Violence often appears in drama lessons because children are exposed to violence on television, in movies, in the news, and even on the streets in a nation where "entertainment" is synonymous with violence. The media teaches that violence solves problems. When Mrs. Allen's news about taking the land away from the Indians disturbed the children in the Potawatomi sessions, two children made guns out of magic markers and shot Mrs. Allen. In

"Prison at the River's Bend," I had planned a caring story a snowman with a guitar, but the kindergarten children were determined to play out a violent story of a robber who stole the guitar.

Even the youngest players care deeply about justice, and teachers must consider the need for poetic justice in the light of nonviolence. One of the major problems of the drama teacher is how to resolve conflicts ethically. Recently I was observing a student teaching a fourth grade class in a local school. The group was making up a story together, each child adding a story around and around the circle. Time and time again, as the story got to a small group of boys across from me, the hero of the story (no matter what else was happening to him) met a policeman and shot him dead. The entire group of twenty-eight children dissolved into laughter. How could these children believe that killing a police officer was funny? Yet we know that in homes all across the United States after dinner, violent acts play out on the television screen at the rate of five to six per hour. A criminal act was perpetrated against one out of every four households in the mid 1990's. We are a violent people with violence in our everyday lives. In 1985 *Dramatics,* the magazine of the International Thespians, listed a catalogue of thirty eight violent plays from the contemporary theatre. This list accompanied an article on how important it is to high school theatre students to be able to stage realistic violence.

But isn't dramatic violence valuable as catharsis?

As theatre workers, we must come to terms with the Greek concept of catharsis as it has been used over the centuries to justify violence in the theatre. Greek plays were about violence, but violent acts were never shown on stage. Aristotle's theory of catharsis contends that being aware of violence through the drama, as in the slaughter of Medea's children, will purge audiences of hostile emotions and make peace in daily lives. Later periods did show violence on the stage; the suicides, for example, in *Romeo and Juliet.*

Modern psychology has fairly well punctured the happy balloon of catharsis. In theatre we have clung to it for centuries, but now we must abandon it as useless to contemporary society. Plainly, Aristotle was wrong. The eminent psychologist, Dr. Jerome Singer, who has devoted much of his life to studying how the mind uses story-making, has stated unequivocally that there is no good violence. Research shows time and again that exposure to violence breeds violence. It is that simple. When exposed to violence, a child from a stable home may not become as violent as a person from an unstable home; but both will become more violent than they were before the exposure.

Carol Tavris, in *Anger, the Misunderstood Emotion*, refers to several studies on responses to anger which support this conclusion. But she insists that people can break the violence cycle. In numerous examples of research and field studies, Tavris notes how subjects have been trained, or even trained themselves to respond to anger constructively. The violence that comes into our homes had been termed "clean violence." The gore, the blood, the suffering, and the irreversibility of it is never presented. The media glosses over the bloody and painful aspects of physical and mental cruelty, while it emphasizes the heroism and excitement of violent acts. It rarely shows the long suffering of victims and those who love them. The criminal Peter Lee Grenier referred to this as he spoke about a crime he committed in 1969. ("On Smashing the Human Skull," *Grand Rapids Press*, April 8, 1984.) He was still in prison in 1983 when he wrote about his experiences. In the course of a gas station robbery, he hit the attendant on the head with the butt of a gun.

> *I was totally nauseated . . . I was first of all terrified that I might have killed him. That was not my intent. It was not my desire — really — to hurt anybody; it was a spontaneous type of violence.*

> *Somehow I was trying to assert my manhood — trying to find out . . . if I could commit violent acts . . . what was seemingly a simple and nearly painless operation on radio and television was much more in reality. It was a nauseating sound of crushed and mushy flesh as the gun butt smashed into the attendant's head and bore through to a solid bone surface, lubricated by the flow of warm blood.*

> *The attendant wasn't dead, but he needed help, and so did I; and so do a lot of other victims of the neatly packaged violence. The problem is not with that which is seen on television, however, but with that which is not seen — the truth about violence.*

One thing that we can do to bring people to the truth of violence in thematic drama is to make it clear that there is no such thing as clean violence. When Mrs. Allen dies, she is gone, and her blood is forever on our hands. When we put a person in jail, we must then take care of that person. When we laugh at a police officer being killed, we must experience the suffering of his family.

In order to break the cycle, we must provide young people that we meet in the drama with techniques for solving problems that are non-violent. What is there to do? We can join organizations, and read books on the subject. We can attend lectures and seminars. Communcation and conflict resolution publications have much to teach on how we can work with players to provide them with win/win situations, solutions which do not pit **us** against **them**. We can take a clue from the British high school teacher who was totally appalled by the Rambo movies. She spent a whole year with her high school classes exploring values that Hollywood continues to foist on British teenagers.

As we work with young people we must become familiar with the creative solutions to problems practiced in other cultures. We can borrow **shunning** from the Amish; we can borrow the **town meeting** from New England; we can borrow the concept of **group responsibility** from the Micronesians; we can understand others through Japanese Pillow Talk. A curriculum for peace has been adopted by many school districts, and it provides useful additional ideas for non-violence in the classroom.

The problems of control and power in the drama room, which are addressed in the next chapter, cannot be completely solved until we face the problem of general violence in our soceity. But when we are steeped in strong values, and armed with the ability to exercise classroom management techniques, perhaps drama can help us in some ways to make all our chaos constructive.

The drama leader has a tight rope to walk. On the one hand, the class needs to be led to consider difficult questions. On the other, the teacher can give her opinions, but she must not impose her ideas and values on the group, even if they express her strongest feelings. Theatre should be an open forum where every possibility can be considered, hence an ideal art form to go hand in hand with freedom of speech. Theatre is most exciting when it poses interesting and complex questions. It is not exciting when it gives pat answers.

Sources

"Catalogue of Violent Plays from the Contemporary Theatre," *Dramatics.* Spring, 1985, p. 27.

COLES, ROBERT. *The Moral Life of Children.* Boston: The Atlantic Monthly Press, 1986.

COX, HARVEY. *Religion in the Secular City: Toward a Postmodern Theology.* New York: Simon and Schuster, 1984.

GILLIGAN, CAROL. *In a Different Voice.* Cambridge, MA: Harvard University Press, 1982.

KANNER, BERNICE. "What Price Ethics? The Morality of the Eighties." *New York*, July 14, 1986, pp. 28 - 34.

KOLBERG, LOUIS. *The Philosophy of Moral Development.* San Francisco: Harper and Row, 1981.

POSTMAN, NEIL. *The Disappearance of Childhood.* New York: Dell Publishing Co., Inc., 1982.

STEELE, EDWARD C. and CHARLES W. REDDING. "The American Value System: Premise for Persuasion," in *The Speaker's Reader.* Ed. Robert L. Scott. Glenview, IL: Scott, Foresman and Co., pp. 52 - 60.

TAVRIS, CAROL. *Anger: The Misunderstood Emotion.* New York: Simon and Schuster, 1982.

GIVING POWER AND KEEPING CONTROL

> *"The process is called entrophy. It's the natural flow of things from order to chaos."*
>
> *Physicist John Hill*
>
> *"All art comes out of chaos."*
>
> *Ellert Ekerdal*

This chapter introduces ways to

- *slow the drama;*

- *handle difficult groups;*

- *and get power out of chaos.*

NOTHING CAN BE GAINED IN VALUES, HOWEVER, if the players are not in a position to receive the drama. In the years that I have been teaching students to use theatre in the classroom, the greatest issue facing the program and the students has been losing and gaining control. Thematic drama gives the power to the players, but it must not let the leader lose control of the group.

There is no doubt that drama is open-ended. It often does not have the homework or the desk work of a math class; nor can it be tested easily and objectively, like reading. Since the benefits and product are often invisible, and since the only visible part may be a room full of players noisily moving about, many people think drama is not a serious endeavor. Because a leader may be told to expect chaos, this in turn can become a self-fulfilling prophecy for a leader. The opposite is also true: the leader who expects players to behave will find serious response in most instances.

A trained leader knows that informal theatre has a very serious mission and intent; but the laughter, the scraping of desks across the floor, and the occasional cries in role can convince the principal, the parents, and fellow teachers that drama is only more recess. Despite this, it must be conceded that there is a limit to the disorder a school system can tolerate. Those who will be doing drama in a community center or in a theatre may have much more leeway to make noise, but they too will want the drama to be more than fun babysitting. Without the leader in control of the situation, serious goals will be impossible to reach.

It takes courage and good reasons to defend the open-ended aspects of drama to colleagues. Leaders must make it clear that noise and emotion are only a very small part of what happens in the drama lesson. If observers look for concentration in individual players, goals to be achieved, and the elaborate planning that goes into achieving them, they may eventually become more tolerant of a little well-placed noise.

If the class is deeply engaged, there will be few control problems. Peter Slade described people actively engaged in the drama as having "absorption." When absorbed, participants are not distracted by anything but another moment in the drama. Slade's term describes a player deeply concentrating on his role and in the situation, not "out of control," or "too loud," but intent upon the objective at hand. Absorption occurs when there is complete concentration on the here and now. But like the formal theatre, not all players will be equally absorbed at any given time. When deep concentration by every member of the group is achieved, creative drama reaches the level of art.

"Creative chaos"

But not all drama can take place quietly at students' desks. Participants have to get up and move about. Often they have to talk. And some emotions will call for loud voices. There cannot be quiet lessons all of the time. There may be times when a drama lesson looks like a mess to an outsider, when actually it is in a constructive and important time of creative involvement for the participants. In fact, the Swedish drama leader Ellert Ekerdal contends that all art comes out of chaos, so we must not fear chaos. Chaos can be constructive, so long as the players are not harming anyone and, more importantly, if within the unstructured time the group endeavors to solve the problems the drama poses. Rapid movements and loud cries in character may even add to absorption.

"The Potawatomis of Pearline" provides several examples of creative chaos. Meta constantly left the group, running off on some errand of her own. But when she returned to the group she usually had made an object, a crown or flower to give to someone — the way she communicated with the group. Reaffirming her attachment, she hugged or touched someone, contributing to her own or to the others' sense of involvement. Although this behavior might have had to be modified in a classroom with twenty-seven other players, in the small group present for these sessions, her actions were accepted by the others, and they helped both her and the others enjoy the moments of the drama.

Nicole, another child in the same class, often made faces into the camera, refused to believe, made fun of the leader and shattered the fragile belief the others were building. She rudely laughed at me and at her fellow students. In the role of Traveling Bluebird it became necessary for me to enlist the group to join in disciplining her. After being "shunned" by the group for ten minutes, she behaved herself for the final five hours of the class, cooperating beautifully, and contributing many original ideas, especially on the final day. Nicole was a child who needed to know just how far she could go.

A third child, Tom, fell in and out of character. He loved to tease me and his sister, the assistant leader. Never mean or overly critical, Tom often went deeply into role, so absorbed that it did not occur to him to monitor his "uncool" behavior. He never had to be spoken to; his transformation to deep work came about naturally as he gained experience and confidence.

Not every child likes the drama, and drama leaders must not blame themselves if they do not reach every child. Recent research shows that children fall into two categories — actors and builders. Builders cannot ever expect to be happiest and most absorbed participants. Two boys about seven years old entered a class against their will, announcing that they had spoiled the lesson with yesterday's teacher, and they were going to do it today. At times they were interested in what the group was doing, but mostly they wanted to yell loudly and run. In time I could have captured their interest, but not in the two-hour demonstration I had agreed to do. Some groups are slow to get involved, and leaders must not be discouraged early in the work.

Every teacher has a personal level of tolerance for disorder. It would be wise for a potential theatre leader to discover just how much chaos can be tolerated. Thematic drama is hard work that takes complete concentration. Leaders must let the group know that they expect to be working hard all the time on the drama lesson and that they expect the same from the group.

Activity must be balanced with reflection and quiet work. Players who are out of character and situation, commenting about the work, and generally interacting with each other out of role do not allow others to reach absorption. Reckless running and screaming are, of course, never helpful. Time devoted to action might well be less than fifty per cent of the total. The reflection process should be no louder than any other lively classroom discussion, and often it may be much quieter. A successful leader must master techniques for getting young people to move willingly from a more active mood to a quieter mood.

Techniques to slow the drama

A slower drama will be a more controlled drama. Here are some techniques to accomplish this:

- A **change in art forms** will slow the drama. A class working on developing a new breakfast cereal was slowed when it stopped planning and began designing the cereal boxes.
- **Civic and religious rituals** also work: a wedding, a funeral.
- **Daily rituals** which hold people's lives together, such as going to sleep and brushing teeth, are also useful.
- **Questions**, as discussed earlier, make the drama deeper and more controlled.
- The leader may pull the lesson together to **summarize** and put labels on experiences, pointing out commonalities that the group may not see.
- The **symbolic prop** also deepens.
- As does **sensory work**. When planning dramas, it is helpful to include

experiences that will appeal to all the senses, as they have great power to draw people together — feeling, tasting, hearing, smelling and touching. Sharing the Kool-Aid "Firewater" in "The Potawatomis of Pearline" brought the group together.

• **Formal occasions** such as Oriental tea ceremony, a British high tea, an awards banquet, a class reunion, all can provide rich sensory experiences for the group.

Does thematic drama require "rules"?

A beginning leader may find it helpful to write a short list of class rules, emphasizing signals for stop and start, giving copies for all concerned. The class may write its own drama code or make laws in role that will aid in concentration. When leaders have more confidence in the process, they may throw out the list and improvise. Strict adherence to the code does establish a standard of behavior. Players appreciate consistency and adjust to the behavior demanded from them.

Leaders may have to stop the drama to discipline a particularly unruly group. Even Dorothy Heathcote occasionally had to do this. There is no sense in going on with a lesson if there is no concentration. Players must not think for a minute that drama is an excuse for running wild. The leader must make it clear to the players that drama is a privilege, one that can be taken away from them at any time that the group shows that they do not have the maturity to work in a flexible structure.

What — walk out in the middle of a lesson?

I have, in a classroom where the students, a group of sixth graders, would not cooperate after I had made several sincere tries. Their classroom teacher had indicated to them through his facial expressions that drama was not to be taken seriously, and the players picked up on it. I felt no qualms about leaving the group and their teacher mid-lesson. In the classroom there are always other activities to turn to if the lesson is not working. Drama leaders are too valuable to be victims. Teachers can turn to some other important activity in the classroom and try drama another day when the group may be ready for its demans.

Those working in community education, recreational and theatre settings are not so lucky as to be able to completely abandon a class. Parents inevitably have dropped the young people off for the announced length of the class. Leaders will have to cope with the problem of continuing a lesson — some lesson. Early in the work with a group, leaders should find some interesting and challenging theatre games that this group of students will like. These will help provide variety and control. Viola Spolin's books of theatre games can be a great resource here. The very strict rules of the games both teach the art of theatre and help leaders set limits. After success in these controlled situations, the leader can move on to lessons with fewer external controls.

One of the very difficult but exciting things about working with groups is that there are never two alike. Even the same group varies in mood from minute to minute. In drama, a lesson that did not work with one group may be a hit with another. A lesson a class rejected one day may be a great success another day. On the other hand, some lessons almost always fail, while others rarely do. There is no formula for how to approach this, except not to get upset when it happens, and to always have a third lesson plan to use if the first two do not work.

Drama specialists attached to school districts have their unique problems of control, going from class to class, seeing a group only once or twice a week, not aware of what has happened in the classroom that week that affect the individuals and the group. It's more difficult to use events from the formal instructional process or from life in the cafeteria or in the playground as the basis of the day's drama.

A group that appears quiet while the regular classroom teacher is present may be functioning only by external control. When the iron hand of that particular teacher is lifted, the players may become the most boisterous group the drama leader has encountered. The players are so delighted to have some freedom that they take the control of the class from the leader. In all cases, the leader must be in tune with the group. It pays to give considerable thought to the daily situation of the players. A leader should plan time to talk informally to them, finding out what amuses them, what excites them, what touches their emotions.

The logistics of space and arrangements

The place you choose to work can affect control. A classroom seems a logical place to work, but often classrooms are cluttered, and it never seems to fail that they are situated next to another class engaged in a quiet activity. Many people must take their classes to the gym for drama. But the gym really does not lend itself to the demands of the play. In the first place, it is the spot where students are used to running, throwing things and yelling in loud voices. The gym usually overwhelms in its vastness and its blazing lights, destroying the intimacy drama lessons require. A fairly empty, medium-sized room with a carpeted floor is ideal. A library, empty classroom, or music room works well. Being able to control the intensity of the light in the room makes it even better suited to creating various moods of the drama work. If the room is somewhat isolated in the building, or in a noisy part of the building, that is even better; for then the active parts of the work will not disturb others.

Drama groups work best in a circle arrangement. This is both natural and comfortable. It avoids the "on stage," "off stage" effect, and it provides a mutual ability for everyone to see everyone else in the room. It does not put anyone in a position of greater emphasis, which tends to encourage showing off. It also does not permit anyone to get lost in the crowd. It is completely democratic.

The most effective control in the lessons comes out of the situations and characters in the drama itself

In teaching through role, power is given to the learner. Through empowerment, seriousness, and problem-solving, players by and large will come to discipline themselves. In "The Potawatomis of Pearline," control came through the warnings of the Great Kinnekinec (a puppet manipulated by the leader) and from being watched by the white scout. In "The Land of the Kish," control was achieved through the necessity to use gibberish (the foreign captives' language). In "Old Charlie," control came through the necessity to keep information limited to a very small group of friends.

Drama must be planned and executed so that every player is actively engaged in play at all times. This is one of the great strengths of drama. There is no waiting in turn; there is no hierachy in the class. Everyone works on the problem at once, and everyone's ideas and work are treated as respectfully as everyone else's. With competition out of the picture, one person's success will not depend upon another's failure. Clear instructions, an atmosphere of work, and limitations, provide the easiest discipline of all.

Edminston, Enciso and King reported in the February, 1987 *Language Arts* that drama in the classroom does empower readers and writers. In the lesson described, students assumed the roles of museum art directors who were developing a display about Christopher Columbus. Through focusing on this problem, the players learned to read more carefully and to write with authority. Excitement about their newly discovered ability to control their environment, and the recognition that they possessed the authority to solve adult problems, made discipline problems a thing of the past.

In thematic drama, students come to know what they know. They know what they are expected to know . . . what they need to know . . . how much they know. They begin to have confidence in themselves. At last they can see a purpose for their accumulated knowledge. They begin to use it to solve problems. They are in power because they have the answers to questions. The leader ensures that they use their power democratically.

Built-in controls

The attitude of the drama leader also contributes to the power of the learner and the control of the leader. The leader must respect the drama and the group's ability to do it. Heathcote detests "artsy" types. She thinks that common people should reclaim theatre from the dominance of the elite, the dilettantes, and those who place spectacle before plot, character or thought. While waiting for a bus in Newcastle, several of her institute students began some theatre warm-ups, saluting the sun, two of them, bending and swaying like dancers. Heathcote commented, "Too much drama has been taught in leotards."

The roles that leaders choose for themselves and the players also can contain built-in controls. Some sections of lessons can be totally silent, using circumstances in life where people cannot speak. They may have laryngitis, may be aged or sick. Sometimes they cannot understand each other because of language barriers. Having the class work in gibberish as a foreign language adds an interesting dimension to the work. The gibberish is so challenging to the players that it can become as attractive as misbehaving.

One of the best ways to have control come out of the story is to build watchers into it. Often there is an unseen enemy in the land, and one must be quiet to keep the enemy at bay. "Shhh. The giant is asleep." "The Nazi's are everywhere on the street, and we must not make any sudden move or in any way look suspicious." Or there may be an internal reason to use silence. "On the way to the ball, silence has always been observed." "We must whisper while the baby is asleep." Stories may be set in a museum, in a raging storm, in the Holy of Holies — all times and places where speech is useless or forbidden.

Leaders should sometimes encourage players to move away from the group, while still maintaining their roles. "Go to your room and pack all of the things you will need for the journey." Or falling asleep can be made a part of the lesson. Asking the players to "go to sleep in your hogans" can be useful for control, as well as for reflection.

Dealing with rowdy boys

Society condones boys at a certain age who incorporate rowdy behavior into their roles. Needless to say, this can get out of hand in a hurry. Louis Kolberg and Vivian Paley have shown us that justice is very important for male children in the elementary grades. Leaders need to devise ways to use this male developmental stage, if for no other reason than to keep their devil-may-care side in check. In a lesson on Inuits, a group of boys pretended to be drunk. In character, the leader, who was playing an elder of the village, chastised the participants soundly for disgracing her honorable people. The rest of the class discussed their embarrassment over the behavior and voted on how to keep the boys from getting out of control again.

Leaders should include the possibility of consequences for those who do not honor the code of silence. Players should "live by the law" the group creates. When there is some questionable behavior, the group develops the punishment for the offender. Police and jails may be used with some groups, although this may be only a last resort. Another possibility is passive punishment, such as practiced in Micronesia, where a whole village takes responsibility for an offender, sitting together with him in the city square.

Groups and regrouping

Breaking the large group into smaller groups often helps with control. It is difficult to problem-solve with twenty seven other people, so groups of four to six can brainstorm and take over various projects, working on their own. This is particularly effective with students over ten years old. The group may do a lot of talking in this arrangement, so leaders must plan ways to keep loud voices to a minimum.

Care must be taken in creating groups, putting students who work well together in the same group. Some people just cannot work together without trouble. In certain grades boys and girls do not want to be close together. It is wise to honor the desire to work with the same sex, but occasionally mixing the sexes aids in maturation. Margaret Chatoor, a secondary teacher in Trinidad and Tobago, names one person in the group as the captain. That person is responsible for the behavior of the group.

Research time, quiet individual thinking, writing, drawing and other planning activities all help to put the lid on rambunctiousness. In the theatre and classroom, often the active and reflective parts of the drama will be balanced with a third component where players consult books, videotapes, and even computer programs in order to bring solutions to the problems posed in role. This work follows the rules of independent learning so familiar in many of today's classrooms that it does not need elaboration.

Other techniques include introducing a non-verbal physical activity for a limited time, or limiting the number of words that can be spoken, or limiting the number of minutes allowed for planning. This helps players control and organize their ideas. The leader may ask players to whisper what they are feeling or thinking. This way players do not copy their answers from others, and they can tell the leader something they might be embarrassed to share with the entire group.

All of us like to be known by our names. It helps the player feel that he or she is an individual whom the leader recognizes. Those who control mobs have taught us that by calling a person by name, that person will begin to think of himself as an individual and start questioning the mob behavior he is engaged in. Leaders should learn each student's name as soon as possible. It may seem silly to play a name game, but it is so important to know names that any method becomes valid.

The "acting out" portion of the story may be accomplished more quietly in many ways. Camera and film are so familiar to players that their terminology and techniques can help with control. Leaders may ask the players to perform active scenes in slow motion, to make a "silent movie," or to "turn the sound down on the TV." These allow excitement without chaos. The leader can use imaginative directions. "I took a movie of what you just did. Show me the movie again, but play it in slow motion." Videotaping the classroom activity affects behavior in the group. Although it may inhibit some, for others the inhibitions may be welcomed.

The leader may also slow the action and minimize the commotion by stopping to have the students set up a frozen dramatic pose. Players can pose for still photos, set up a wax museum, do storytelling. A good rule for reenactment is that it is often more selective than the original — what we call "selected realism." A whole event cannot be lived through. The task of the drama leader is to carefully choose those parts encouraging concentration and depth.

With all the fundalmentals of thematic drama well in control, you are now in shape to try some lessons of your own.

Sources

EDMISTON, BRIAN, PAT ENCISO, and MARTHA L. KING. "Empowering Readers and Writers Through Drama: Narrative Theatre." *Language Arts*, 64:2 (February), 1987, pp. 219 -228.

SPOLIN, VIOLA. *Improvisation for the Theatre*. Evanston: Northwestern University Press, 1963.

STRUCTURING THEMATIC LESSONS AND CREATING SCENARIOS

"I find when I plan too much, I do not listen to the children."

Cecily O'Neill

This chapter introduces

• *beginning a drama;*

• *creating roles;*

• *using plot strategies;*

• *and deepening the work.*

THEATRE RESEMBLES LIFE in that it is often lived first and understood later. Despite this, the leader of the drama must infuse theatre experiences with the potential for meaning. Dramas have meaning on several levels, all of which the drama leader needs to address. Content can relate to standard school subjects: literature, geography, history, or material created especially for the class. Interpersonal and intrapersonal development is both the subject of theatre and its mode of address. The personal intelligences, therefore, are integrated into the action at the same time they provide working techniques. The drama, then, is about sharing, participation, cooperation, sensitivity and problem solving as well as it displays these characteristics.

The characteristics of the art of theatre also need to be taught. These include such dramatic elements as plot, character, and environment. Not every lesson has to include each of these categories of goals or their subpoints, but they provide a rich menu from which to choose.

Once goals are established, it is important to step back and examine specific parts of the lesson which must be planned ahead of time. These are:

• A theme to be addressed

• A spine of action which may take place

• Several situations which can be used to explore the theme

• A clear understanding of the dramatic elements which will make this theatre event emotionally satisfying

• Roles for the players and leader(s)

• An incident to start the improvisation

Where do you get ideas for a playable action?

Everywhere! In fact, once the leader becomes familiar with how to look for them, ideas will pop up all around: in one's personal life, in the newspapers, in history, in literature, in considering values and sense of right and wrong. Round robin story-telling can provide inspiration for the group. Creative writing projects often inspire drama work. Dreams provide powerful raw material for the drama, and are especially useful in getting fantasy into the work. The simple story-telling found in "Prison at the River's Bend" provided bountiful ideas for the group to explore. As they look about themselves, experienced leaders find themselves saying, "I must do a drama lesson about that soon."

SOURCES FOR THE DRAMA

1. Events as a source

    Current events

    Family stories

    Performance arts events

2. Objects as an action source

    Stories can be acted out based on an arrangements of objects

    A drama could be built on a prop

    A costume can be an inspiration for drama

    Masks can inspire a scenario

I may set up a "still life" of objects on and around a chair. A rose, for instance, a playing card, a necktie, a ripped picture, some play money, and an open Bible. Then we look at the still life and talk about the possibilities. Who lives here? What has happened? What will happen? I use it somewhere in the drama to heighten the suspense or to explain a scene that may be too shocking to play out.

3. Traces of a character

    A character's costume parts

    A character's possesions

    Odors can suggest character

4. Literature

5. History

6. Formula beginnings, such as "Once upon a time, in a kingdom far away . . ."

7. Dreams

8. Madness

9. Ghosts

10. Omens

11. Fortune telling

12. Letters

After a theme is chosen, the leader will have her moment of creativity as she produces a host of images, forms, plots and characters appropriate to explore this theme. The remainder of this chapter addresses ways to approach this creative experience.

All drama grows out of conflict

Conflict is central to the plan. Who is at odds with whom? Is the struggle between individuals? Little people against the mighty? Two groups in conflict? Is this about ordinary people struggling through natural disasters?

Character roles come out of tensions. Usually the class members play the progatonists. The leader may have to play the antagonist, the hero's nemesis. But it is better to have the antagonist be only an insignificant role for the leader, because the leader cannot guide the action from a morally wrong point of view. Often the antagonist never appears, but only makes threats from afar. If two leaders are working with the group, one of the leaders can play the antagonist, and the other can be on the side of the protagonists, as Tammy Holmden and I did with "The Potawatomis of Pearline."

An extended thematic drama may have several forms of conflict. In the drama of the Potawatomis, the big people, the Great White Fathers in Washington, D.C., take the land of the Indians through a treaty over which the Indians have had little or no control. The Potawatomi lessons are also about powerless people harming other powerless people. The white settlers push the Indians out of their land. The Indians immediately, without discussion or attempt to compromise, take up arms and kill. Natural catastrophe comes to the Indians when they encounter quicksand and illness in the journey to Lowell.

"Getting the angle"

Once the conflict emerges, it is desirable to find an approach to the lesson that is indirect. Newspaper writers call this "getting an angle." Cecily O'Neill used the indirect method when in "The Three Little Pigs," she came to the house built of bricks as the postman. A teacher of religious drama had an angle when in the role of one of Noah's neighbors, she told the players that Noah was out of his mind to build an ark when the sun was shining.

An angle on the story will help students to distance themselves from the events so that they are able to play a thoughtful drama as well as an emotional one. In "Walk like an Egyptian," seven and eight year olds played curators at a new museum where they set up a display of "ancient Egyptian statues." This angle to the story solved the problem of pretending to be preoccupied with the after life, as were the actual Egyptians. At the same time, the brotherhood of all who have walked with a distinct posture could be explored.

The angle chosen must be interesting, and the structure must allow the excitement to build. In a lesson about a land-fill case, a court trial between citizens and a chemical company might be the point the drama is approaching.

After all, that is where the great tension lies. But if the first thing that appears in the lesson is the trial, the work will be shallow. Scenes exploring the problem must be included to help the players develop strong opinions. There must be enough time working in role for the players to believe in their roles, as well as understand the intellectual content. Only after belief has been built, and the situation understood, can the trial develop effectively.

Some distancing techniques may be helpful

These include

• Narration to move the action

• Several alternative endings

• Several points of view at once

• Skips in time and place.

These techniques work in informal drama as well as in a formal play. For example, some Norwegian drama leaders wanted to introduce an understanding of child abuse to young people. Rather than work with a contemporary story or news item, they decided to distance the theme by using the childhood of Hitler. A leader who wants players to understand the AIDS epidemic better might lead a drama about the plague. Heathcote discovered that by presenting history through archeology or art, players worked more deeply than when they went back to the time itself. Distancing is a useful tool, but it must not nullify desirable identification with time, place and person.

At first glance, some subjects may not seem especially appropriate for a theatre lesson. Safety — raising or lowering the driving speed — is an example. Yet there are ways to handle even that. A clue comes from thinking about which people might have an interest in this decision. Who wants the speed higher? Who wants it at 55? What experiences made the characters think the way that they do? Have they been in accidents themselves? Do they need to save gas? How can a person gather statistics to show that 65 is as safe as 55? How do people get others to support their point of view? How do they get their ideas into law?

The "inciting incident"

Cecily O'Neill says the first few minutes of a drama lesson are the most important. Scholars of drama agree. Theorists have isolated a moment at the beginning of a play that they call the "inciting incident." This incident sets the plot in motion, causing first one thing to happen that in turn will cause other happenings.

It is important in planning a lesson to discover something that will provide the inciting incident early, to arrest the attention of the group as it starts to work. Although the first words the leader speaks to the group may have to do with control and the need for suspending disbelief, the second words have to be something to bring the players into the activity, posing a problem or exploring such a unique point of view that the group is ready to throw themselves into the story. Heathcote calls this "hooking the children into the problem."

To start a drama about "Goldilocks" with young children, the leader might ask in the role of a law officer, "Have you seen a little girl with yellow hair? This is the house of the Bears, isn't it? Mrs. Harris thought you might have seen her."

To begin "Passage on the Anne," I came into the room with a battered bundle under my arm in great excitement saying, "Look! The letters from Plymouth Colony have arrived. Mistress Brown, this looks like a letter for you. (*Hands it out.*) Captain Arlin, here is something for you." And so on and on until all of the variety of worn envelops were distributed. Some of the assembled players did not hear from their relatives. "What have you found out?" I whispered to two or three who have letters, fearing that some may contain sad news as well as good news of loved ones.

The lesson with college students about life on the Oregon Trail began with the distribution of handbills describing the opportunities in the West for women. In the role of a friendly neighbor I suggested that each person send a letter of application to the address on the bill. The players began their work by writing a letter of inquiry to the boss of the wagon train.

In addition to the structural reasons for doing so, jumping into the story immediately is life-like and it adds mystery. By moving directly into the action, the players make the story their own. Not only must this first moment of the drama get the attention of the participants, but it must focus attention and put the group into a problem-solving mode. The attention arrestor needs to be something that the group has rarely or never thought of before, something which is challenging for the age level, yet within the possibility of the group. Big moments may be interspersed later in the lesson when it is important to startle and bring the group back together with excitement. I did that with the arrival of Traveling Blue Bird the medicine woman and her bird Kinnekinec in "The Potawatomis of Pearline." But later inciting incidents will never be as important as they are at the top of the story.

The beginning of a drama may take a fairly long narrative description. Sometimes one or two minutes of monologue from the leader are needed to get the group going. The leader may then make a transformation by saying, "I am going off a little way, and when I come back we will begin the drama. See if you can tell from the clues that I give you who you are and where you are." The leader then might come back and say, "I have been to the top of the mountain, and there is no water or food in sight. Does anyone have an idea what to do?"

It might take most of the first hour to get a group going. The important thing is not to give up too soon. Cecily O'Neill says, "In the early part, I own much of the show."

It might be useful to plan more than one attention arrestor for the day's lesson. A quiet, shy group may need a different opening from a boisterous one. A sarcastic group may need a different opening than an innocent group. Older groups may need something different from younger ones. Consider all of these aspects of the group before beginning. Extra openings planned now will not be wasted. They can be put away for another day.

Here are two attention arrestors from university students. The first one began with a letter to a group of pirates:

> "Now that we burried the dead including our fine captan, we're goin' to have to decide what to do next. I hope those yellow dog pirates that blasted our ship from under us sink from all the treasure they is a haulin. Its only fortunate for us we were close to this here island. Now you all know me, I ain't no leader like our captan, I'm a cook. It looks like those of us who are left could be stranded, but I just don't know what to do . . . any iders?"

and

> "I have climbed to the crow's nest again and looked through the telescope. There is no land in sight. We all know that our food and fresh water rations are almost gone. What are we going to do? I've just come from the captain's cabin. He is still unconscious from that blow to the head he received in yesterday's battle. I know some of us are injured too, but it's going to be up to us to sail this ship home safely. How are we going to do that?"

Creating effective and appropriate roles

Choosing a role for the leader(s) is one of the most important parts of developing a drama lesson. It is especially difficult to find roles which are strong for the children while the leader is in a "not knowing" role. Players must be able to assume the "mantle of the expert." On the other hand, the leader must not be in a position to lose control of the group. Sometimes the leader cannot predict what will be too strong or too weak for a new group. "In the Land of the Kish" I thought that I was presenting a weak character, but the children gave me power. I then became a person to rebel against. Players look for an antagonist as well as a protagonist. The role of Mrs. Brewster in "Passage on the Anne" proved to be a good balance between not knowing and having some good questions. Whatever the role, the leader should be full of questions, not answers.

In order to make a drama from an event, story, or play, you may deviate from the original with no worry. There is no moral obligation to play the story just as it has always been told. Shakespeare, Moliere and all of the great world dramatists have taken old stories and made them serve their own purposes, so why can't you? In "Passage on the Anne," Mr. Weston was an historical figure, but Mistress Brewster was a made-up character. In the Potawatomi lessons, all but the barest facts were followed. The facts of Gandhi's march to the sea are correct in "Indian Salt Belongs to India," but the friends of the marchers and the incidents along the march are fictionalized.

On the whole, students will develop their own roles. British drama leader Brian Way suggests that children often do not want to play beautiful characters. Whether it is inadequacy, embarrassment, or boredom, they much more easily identify with the less beautiful, even the ugly. It is not surprising to find players rebelling against the beautiful, although some players may crave it. Leaders need to be aware that that they may have trouble convincing young people to perform the roles of perfect characters. The great dramas have few "perfect" characters, and it behooves drama leaders to invent flawed characters like the ones in world drama and in life.

It is also important for leaders to heed student's suggestions for roles that they want. Even if the role seems very far from the player's own life, the desire needs to be taken seriously. In a class that has many meetings, leaders need to encourage students to discover several type of roles. Natural leaders do not always have to play leaders. A situation can make a person a leader. This happened in "Walk Like an Egyptian," with the boy who refused to participate as a statue. When he became the inspector of the exhibition, he was content and took the job earnestly, moving statues subtly and quitly. Other players accepted his authority. In the proper role he had no problem with participation or absorbtion.

Strategies for developing the material

Cecily O'Neill's book, *Drama Strategies*, abounds in examples of drama techniques that will help leaders and players reach predetermined goals. Following is a list of techniques O'Neill uses, combined with others that I have developed. They will help the beginning leader see how to turn an idea into a drama.

You may use strategies such as gibberish, improvised scene work, and formal written scenes from existing theatre. Techniques for scene development include **teaching in role**, using the **mantle of the expert**, and creating **tableaux**.

A **tableau** is a frozen picture. Characters may speak or not. Sometimes a player will speak for another character. There are many variations on the tableau: family photos, photos in a gallery, wax-works, Disneyland holograms, illustrated text, living story boards, living cartoons, store window mannequins, statues in the park, and the VCR on "Pause."

There are techniques for deepening tableau work. An observer group many develop titles for another group's tableaux. The tableaux players may accept or reject the titles, giving their reasons. Observers may re-arrange the tableaux. The players may explain why this arrangement conveys the original ideas better or more poorly than the first arrangement. The observers may question those in the tableaux about their characters, what will happen next, what they are thinking now. The characters in the tableaux must answer without changing body position. Observers may make up lines for those in the tableaux to speak. Either the observers or the players may say these lines. Players in the tableaux may say their thoughts. Tableaux are such excellent strategies that there is a temptation to use them too much.

The drama may include spontaneous **discussion.** I once led a lesson about a group of young women who were taken to an island by their radical feminist mothers when they were very young. In the second session the daughters discovered four shipwrecked little boys. The women had to decide what to do with the boys — show their mothers, kill them, send them off to die, or hide them and care for them and love them. The discussion that centered around this problem was some of the most interesting I have ever heard in a drama.

After an active part of the drama, the leader can call for half-group feedback. In this activity, players may be paired with a partner, but only one of the partners is allowed to speak. In a variation of this, only one-half of the group is allowed to talk while the other half listens.

Interviews of all kinds can be used — formal, informal, in twos, small groups, and whole groups. Interviews may copy various television or journalistic styles. The story can become part of the evening news. The talk show interview is also a possibility. The group can be divided into pairs who are best friends. The "best friends" talk over the problem, the characters, a solution.

One of my favorite techniques is the "**hot seat.**" In the hot seat, one player sits in front while other players ask questions. The player must answer in character, making up answers as he or she goes along. The answers the hot-seated person gives add to character, playable action, and environment. In a series of lessons on AIDS, one of the leaders of the group played Magic Johnson's wife. She was asked a number of questions about her life:

"Do you still love Magic?"
"Are you afraid for yourself? Your baby?"
"Where do you live?"
"Does your mother have any thoughts about this situation?"
"You are pretty rich. How has this affected your pocketbook?"
"Did you approve of Magic quitting the President's Council?"

The answers gave the group many possible situations to play together, helping them to better understand the emotional level of what it means to be HIV Positive.

Players may share **inner monologues** verbally or in writing. They can make drawings: story boards, cartoons, murals. They can "sign in" to class by writing something on a large roll of paper.

In addition to these more informal ways of structuring lessons, eventually leaders like to use some **more formal episodes**. The best episodes are set in public: a court house, a 4th of July celebration, the park, etc., and the idea to be dramatized has to relate to the group. One group worked on a story about the first woman running for president of the United States. A few members of her nearest family knew that she was born outside of the United States — something even she did not know. At a family picnic the old aunts slowly circled around the group and whispered the news. Should the family suppress this news or reveal it to the candidate — or the press?

Scenes do not have to move chronologically from A to B. They may start in the middle, go to an early part in the story, and then go to the end. The drama is always in the "here and now," but it can move forwards, backwards, or sideways in its evolution. This is an old movie technique, "Meanwhile, back home at the ranch." A character, subject or situation is often explored to its best advantage by moving the story forward 10, 20, or even 30 years. The character of Charlotte in "Honoring Charlotte," is analyzed in depth easily by working on what things would be appropriate to do to make her memory live on. In moving forward the leader can plan statues, exhibits, television shows and other activities.

When tackling a large subject, such as the long life of a great person, you may play only the great moments. The group may play the background to that moment, what O'Neill calls "the bit before the bit." What came before Edison got the sound out of the phonograph? What came before Amelia Earhart's last flight? Players may reenact the inciting incident — the moment that got the story going. The leader and players together can make a time line of a story and the players may decide on the points to dramatize.

The leader can create scenes not "in" the original story or play. What is the incident that could be terrible enough to make the Montagues and Capulets such mortal enemies for generations? What was the courtship of the Gibbs, the parents in *Our Town*, like? How did George go on after Emily's death?

Giving depth, intellectually and emotionally

As theses episodes are played out, the leader strives to deepen the drama. This can be accomplished in several ways, some of which have been discussed before. The story can stop while the group reflects on the content and the form. How do the players like the way things are developing? Is there something more they would like to explore? Do they want to skip over other parts? The pace of the drama can be slowed. Going backwards in the story or sideways to "the ranch" does that. The causes of the current circumstances can be explored. Perhaps someone else's point of view can be developed.

The drama leader may impose rituals. Learning the dance as a beginning to the last day of the "Potawatomis of Pearline" did just that. A wedding can be celebrated, a funeral staged, a graduation reenacted. Questions can be posed either in or out of role to help the group think and discuss the problem or the form.

Integrating other art forms also deepens the work. Leaders should be aware of symbols and the use of metaphor. They may bring in symbols, often in the form of props or other scenic devices. These should be fully explored by the players who, in turn, may be encouraged to add and share symbols.

Here are some common errors that beginners tend to make as they plan thematic theatre lessons:

- The material may be too difficult or too babyish
- Roles for the leader may be too strong
- Lessons may be dominated by leader talk or the talk of one or two players
- There are not enough internal controls built into the story
- The drama is used to teach specific facts, not to provide an experience in the brotherhoods through drama.

What about failure?

The leader should not worry too much about it. Experiences are experiences, and human beings learn as much or more from "bad experiences" as from "good experiences." There is no need to worry about saving face in front of the players. Inevitably they will have "got something" out of the drama. The good times will outnumber the bad, and everone knows that batting .500 is excellent. When we ask ourselves how many unsuccessful math lessons we have sat through, we can get some perspective on the amount of leeway there is in any teaching. Art is built on opposites: action cannot be appreciated without significant pause, and pleasure cannot be appreciated without pain.

In the dramatic mode, one cannot work on one thing at a time. The juices have to flow. As playwright Virginia Koste has said about informal drama, "It is not the expectancies that I am looking for in the drama, but the unexpectancies." By definition, theatre is a gestalt. If there is not a gestalt, there is not theatre. Drama, like life, follows deductive reasoning. Much as one has an experience, and then asks what can be learned from it, theatre does the same thing. Benefits may not be able to be determined before or even during the event.

A form and check list for planning a thematic theatre lesson appears in the Appendix. This may be helpful to the beginning drama leader. The form does not ask for specific outcomes, but emphasizes goals and the beginning.

As leaders begin making plans, I give you O'Neill's word of caution: "Too much attention to the plan may encourage the leader to stop taking clues from the players." Ultimately, most of the planning for a drama lesson must take place while the lesson is in full swing and the leader is on her feet. We now turn to that dynamic — samples of experiences in leading the players as the improvisation progresses.

Sources

KOSTE, VIRGINIA. *Dramatic Play: Rehearsal for Life*. New Orleans: Anchorage Press, 1982.

THE POTAWATOMIS OF PEARLINE
A Drama Based on Local History

Group: 10 Children from the community aged 8 and 9

Leaders: Laura Gardner Salazar

               College students Tammy Holmden and Pat Sandberg

Time: 5 days for 2 hours per day during July

Space: The university television studio classroom

Michigan history was chosen as the topic for this drama as it was Michigan's 150th year of statehood. Our goals were

Content Goals: To find out what it might have been like to have lived in Michigan 150 years ago.

                     To come into contact with another society

Group Goal: To make some new friends.

Drama Goals: To use spectacle and character to explore another time.

                     To explore how drama is a celebration.

Tensions: Persons in untamed natural surroundings

                     Two groups of people claiming one space

Our planning began with research (see bibliography at end of chapter). From reading about the Potawatomi Indians living in what is now Allendale, Michigan, I made notes on material we might use in the drama:

- The Metea and Winnemac-Maumee Treaty, 1817, pushed the Indians off their land.

- In the St. Mary's Negotiations, 1817, Indians ceded their lands to the white men for whiskey.

- "The plowshare is driven through our tents before we have time to carry out goods and seek another house."

- Some reserves, small tracts of land, were saved.

- Some Indian/French mixed families served as go-betweens.

- There was considerable trade between whites and Potawatomis. Most Potowatomis were hunter/trappers, but grew some corn.

- There were problems with alcohol.

- Potawatomis rejected farming. Trading was a more desired goal for them.

- They became Catholics — at least in name.

- Allendale was first called Pearline by its white settlers.

Roles:	Myself — Mrs. Allen, Traveling Bluebird, Senator Gardner
	Tammy — Princess Sunflower (Grandmother)
	Pat — U.S. Army Scout

Materials:	Bird puppet	Blackboard
	Blue Books (Empty test booklets)	
	Bluebird figure	Blue flowers
	Books on Potawatomis	Cups
	Cymbals	Drink
	Film boxes	Food
	Game supplies	Glue
	Markers	Medicine woman costume
	Musical instruments for ceremony	
	Newsprint	Pencils
	Popcorn	Play money
	Role of paper 4' X 6'	String/Yarn
	Treasure for necklaces	U.S. Cavalry hat
	Senator costume	

Although several other children dropped in from time to time, the regulars were

> Tommy, 10, the oldest in the group, boistrous, loves to tease and is very confident because he is the brother of one of the student leaders

> Keith, 9, a quiet, serious boy;

> Kris, 9, equally quiet;

> Meta, 8, very social, bright, creative and curious, with a short attention span;

> Kira, 9, a quiet girl who liked to work for long periods on her own projects;

> Nichole, 9, who came to the lessons because she "wants to be a movie star."

DAY ONE

PLANS

A group of Potawatomi Indians and a Chippewa woman whose husbands work as furtrappers on the Grand River, are setting up a summer fishing camp here on what is now Grand Valley State University property. Among them is a wise old Indian woman, the daughter of a chief, and one of the council of elders named Princess Sunflower.

A white woman named Mrs. Allen comes to ask for help to plant her garden. She has just moved here. Her husband is cutting down trees. They plan to stay and become farmers. Or maybe they will be moving on to other lumbering areas. They may buy a section of land from the government. Mrs. Allen's husband drives a load of lumber down the river to the saw mill. He stays overnight to do some trading. Mrs. Allen sees a wolf prowling around the cabin. She is frightened. The group will begin making their necklace name tage of yarn and empty plastic film cans.

Introduction to the drama

The leaders and children are introduced, and we tour the space, a School of Communications tv studio. I talk about how to use it without getting hurt or breaking anything. I tell the players that the third step of a ladder is safe to jump from. They all try it. "Drama is work by pretending," I begin. "We don't put on a play." I tell the group that they will be studying the Indians in Michigan. Tommy comments, "We've studied this in school hundreds of times. Is it boring in school." I add that the group is going to explore what it would be like to have some land and then to have it taken away. When the group begins to talk about the way to solve this problem by using guns to run off anyone who takes the land away, I ignore them. "When I turn around, I will be in the story," I begin.

The drama as played

The class as Indians begins by spearing sturgeon in the river. Tammy, as Old Princess Sunflower, gives all of the players presents, plastic film boxes on yarn "necklaces." These become receptacles for treasures throughout the week. The group decorates their boxes.

As the group works, they talk about their situation. Tammy mentions that she has seen white people at the trading post. At this point, Meta refers to her as "Majesty," but Tammy explains that she is not a majesty, only a friend who needs help. She asks the group to take her to the river to fish, which they promptly do with jumping and stabbing movements.

The players return to the campsite with huge loads of fish where they pantomime cutting up and cooking their catch, cutting themselves and burning their fingers in the preparation. Others collect berries. The group has some difficulty using imaginary props, and they pick up art supplies and use some of them for imaginary berries. After dinner, story telling is suggested and a round-robin story begins. Meta gets bored and leaves. She comes back to the group and suggests that it is time for sleep.

I call "curtain," and the group gathers out of role to discuss what has happened so far. "What things must all people have?" I ask, moving the group on to the next step. The players answer that all people must have food, clothing, air, water, love, families, etc. I suggests that the play will be about some of these things. "What would you like to work on first?"

Although the girls want to work on love and family, together the whole group agrees that nature is also a good selection; and I promise that even if "nature" will be the major point of attention, "love" and "family" will also be important. I announce that I will turn my back, and when I turn around I will not be one of the Indians any more, but a white person, Mrs. Allen, who has recently moved into the neighborhood.

"Oh, I am so happy to see you. I was all alone last night, and my husband told me that if I had troubles I could come to you. What I have to ask you is how do you handle wolves? Last night I know I heard one outside my door. It didn't howl or anything, but it made that sniffing noise. *(I demonstrate.)* Should I be afraid?"

"What are you doing here?" Tommy asks.

"Chopping down trees."

"Well, don't chop down trees!" Meta cries.

"Don't chop down trees!" they all echo.

"Oh," is Mrs. Allen's only answer. At this point, the group begins to share with each other and Mrs. Allen how they should cope with the wolves. Later she asks about how to grow corn and confesses that she has no idea how to raise a garden in such a cold climate. "Where I am from, it was warm all the time."

The players spontaneously begin helping Mrs. Allen, some working on solving the wolf problem, others on the garden. "Do you know how to trap with a net?" they ask, immediately falling into the action. With drawing materials they begin to demonstrate and explain ways to trap wolves. "We'll show you how to spear fish, too." they add, taking Mrs. Allen to the part of the room where the river has been played.

They add details to the work. "See the terrible cut I got from my spear?" Nicole begins to make prop spears by fitting felt-tipped markers together, end to end. Joyful spearing takes place. At Meta's insistence, the group gets lost, with Meta's map saving the day. Spears forgotten, the group runs about in abandon. Had this been any larger group, spirits could not have run so high, but there is no one to disturb in the building, and the shouting and running added to the story. I tell them that it is time to think about Tuesday.

"That time went fast," Tommy announces. I question the group about which of the segments they had covered. They name family, jobs, food, friiends, and love. Some things not on the list include helping others, health, and good deeds. Each player is to bring a treasure to put in the film box tomorrow.

COMMENTS

The first day seems to have got off to a good start. The children are interested in the subject and are getting along well with each other. They are anxious to join in the activities and are adding greatly to the development of plot and character.

DAY TWO

GOALS

- To build identification with each other and the Indian and White cultures. To continue to help Mrs. Allen.

- To grapple with problems of displacement. To understand character through names bestowed on people.

PLANS

Greet children. Collect their treasures and give them to Princess Sunflower. Introduce blue books (empty test booklets) as a source for expression. Ask children to write something about the experience if they wish. Give finished books to Princess Sunflower, who then will "name" each person. (She will plan this while the rest of the group plans the garden.) Out of role, the group will list things to plant. Then, in role, everyone will plant (draw on large rolled paper) the items they suggested for the garden. Tammy will help as Princess Sunflower only if necessary. Tammy will bestow the names on the people. There will be a naming ceremony with great pomp. The players may make new names to put on their treasure necklaces or show in another way. Mrs. Allen needs the Indians to help in her garden. Mr. Allen will say they must leave. They will not want to leave.

SCENES PLAYED THIS DAY

- Journal work for naming
- Planning the garden
- The crowning of Princess Sunflower
- Plans are finished
- Land prepared
- Putting the garden in place
- Naming ceremony
- Name changes
- Sleep
- Bad news from Mrs. Allen
- Bad news for Mrs. Allen

The drama as played by the children

Jody and Holly, friends of two other girls in the group, join this day. Although they do not assume leadership roles, they are very cooperative and concentrate on the drama. Tommy stays at home. The student leader is late, and the group decides to hide her treasure box from her. She comes in shortly and finds it immediately. Although the mystery is easily solved, it gives the players an opportunity to have some fun together as a group. I announce that

Princess Sunflower is going to give each of them a name. "Go off in a corner and do some thinking." They take their books and writing for five minutes. Princess Sunflower then takes the treasures and books to ponder and name. The players turn their attention to Mrs. Allen's garden. On the blackboard they list things they should plant in the garden, and then the players "make" the garden by drawning it on a large piece of craft paper with magic markers.

Now I appear as Mrs. Allen, and the players invite me to the naming ceremony. Meta constructs a crown out of gold paper and asks Princess Sunflower to close her eyes, as she puts the crown on her head. During the rest of the week, Princess Sunflower will always be seen in her paper crown. (Anachronisms like this were allowed because of the youth of the players and the need to continue in the imaginative world.)

The players take over the garden building as Mrs. Allen asks, "What color will these flowers be?" "Do I need fertilizer?" "What tools do I need?" "How close together should these carrots be?"

For the naming ceremony the group sits in a circle, with Nicole holding her life-sized doll, which become the baby of the village, often passed around and fussed over. Tammy has written a paragraph telling each person in detail his name's significance. Meta receives the name "Cousin Tweeter," because she said that she was related to the Princess. I am given the name "Traveling Bluebird" because of my love for the color blue, my love of birds, and my passion for travel.

Mrs. Allen appears and announces that the Indians will have to move from their village, because her husband has purchased the land. The players laugh. They say that this is ridiculous. They have a long talk over what has to be done. Here are some of the questions I used for building depth:

• How would you feel if your husband told you to ... ?

• But is a weapon the only way?

• Why are you laughing at me?

• Why are you pointing your guns at me?

They deliberate. "Well, are we going to have a war?"

• "We have our rifles."

• "We are not going to let Mr. Allen do this!"

• And Meta sums it up, "How would they feel if we took their land?"

Two of the players, Nicole and Meta, pick up their felt tipped marker "spears" and they proceed to shoot Mrs. Allen many times. They announce that they have also killed Mr. Allen and all the white people around. The rest of the group does not participate and casts disgusted looks at the two rebel girls. Day two ends, and the group cleans up the room and leaves.

LEADER'S COMMENTS

This day saw a variety of subject matter explored. The garden grew as the players invested more time in the project. This activity also built belief. The drama suffered from lack of tension. However, the slow pace of the lesson aided in bonding the group. Students started to ask each other for help. They built trust in the adults. I fussed over the village "baby," and Tammy grew into her crown. At times leaders were too teacherly and gave answers instead of using problems to open areas of interest. The group seemed reluctant to commit to physical work. This is not typical behavior, but this was a very small group, and they had only been together a short time. Also individual differences account for some of the reluctance. The older children are more self-consicous, and the camera made a difference. Also these are precocious children, and their sophistication is evident.

DAY THREE

GOALS:

- To explore what it means to take another's life.

- To explore what it is to live as a fugitive.

- To try to bring the players back together into one group again.

- To seek help from a supernatural being.

- To enjoy puppetry.

PLANS:

Mrs. Allen's animals need tending and the garden is overgrown. Her body needs to be buried. The payment for the land comes to the Potawatomis. There will be celebration, dancing, singing and merrymaking. They have several choices: (1) face the consequences and go to jail; (2) run away and hide; (3) try to live the white people's life; (4) move west and join other Indians.

The drama as played

The work to date is reviewed. Someone in the group wants the next part to be about "water." One person mentions that "love" had not been played, but the leader reminds them of the friendships that had developed between the Princess, Mrs. Allen and the group.

As the doll is present again, and Kira has brought a huge teddy bear, the leader mentions that "family" is important. When asked what should be added to the list, Meta says with a wicked smirk, "Bad deeds."

"Divide into families of two or three," I say. "Plan what your house looks like. Write in your book about your family relationship and draw a picture of your house." The boys make one family while the girls split up into three families. Friends find places apart where they write and draw in their books for several minutes. I leave the room, and Princess Sunflower calls a meeting of the group.

Shortly I appear as Traveling Bluebird. The players refuse to believe that this is not Mrs. Allen returned. I promise to bring proof that I am the old Indian and not the white woman. I bring the news that the Great White Father in Washington has booze and dollars for them to pay for their land. As an official messenger to several tribes, I bring a partial payment to them. While the drinks (Kool-Aid) are being distributed amid a discussion of the power of the "fire-water," Bluebird notices that Sunflower has put the money in her own pocket. "I have seen killing. I have seen rudeness. These pople do not deserve money," she says in defense of her actions. The players object, and Princess Sunflower reluctantly gives out one third of the payment.

Nicole becomes disruptive. I ask if the group will stop talking to Nicole and completely ignore her for ten minutes. They agree to do this. The punishment works, and Nicole is cooperative for the rest of the week.

"Who's taking care of the Allen's farm?"

"Nobody."

"Everybody." Both suggestions pass without comment.

Travelng Bluebird announces that she must sleep, for she has to begin her long walk to Traverse City tomorrow. In actuality, I go behind a screen where I don a shiny ragged black costume, a black floppy hat to cover my face, and a rooster rod puppet made of glittery black feathers with a shiny red comb.

Princess Sunflower says that she too will go to bed, and asks the boys to please keep watch. They discover that the Traveling Bluebird is missing. "Look!" "Come on!" they cry.

With a great crash of cymbals they hear a booming voice. "Stay away from the Medicine Woman!" The players turn and scream, then stand and watch.

"I bring you answers to your problems."

"Why do you come?"

"I come because the Potawatomis are in trouble. Traveling Bluebird told me you were in great trouble. The rooster Kinnekinec comes from the Great Spirit. In order for the bird to speak, he must hear from you about how great it is."

"I will sit and tell you."

"Look there is a big bat!" This is Tommy joining in the game.

"Yes. It is a bat. Sit there and Kinnekinec will catch it. Make sounds and we will catch the bat."

"Now," chants Bluebird as the medicine woman in an eerie voice, "I will tell you all you have to know. You have killed Mrs. Allen, and the consequences will last all of your lives and the lives of your children and your children' children. But I will guide you and protect you and be with you. Cooperate with me. When there is another treaty with the White Father in Washington, all Potawatomis must go to the pow wow. Further, you must listen to the princess. Remember, I bring you good luck. I fought the terrible bat. Farewell." She disappears.

The players wander about—dazed by the appearance of the strange woman in black, talking softly to each other about the experience. Traveling Bluebird is found in a trance, weakly calling, "Help me." Bluebird confesses that sometimes she goes into a deep trance where she is able to help others. The players have a gentle, quiet, almost loving moment. Bluebird talks about how trances make her weak and hurt her head. Meta holds Bluebird's head, swaying it ever so softly. The doll is passed from person to person, each giving it tender caresses. Love has become a part of the lesson. Tommy faints.

The players ask if Bluebird could call Kinnekinec again. Meta and Kira dress the weakened Bluebird in the medicine woman costume. But Kinnekinec seems limp as he speaks. Meta strikes the cymbal before each question. "Will any of us die?" someone asks the rooster.

> "Some will. Some will lose land. You may move down river to Lamont. There is still land there. Do not bring weapons. Do not perform any act which will send you to prison. Traveling Bluebird was imprisoned and almost died of disease there. I am growing weaker and weaker and must go to sleep."

All sleep. When they wake Traveling Bluebird says good-bye to the people. They stumble onto some quicksand but save themselves. Five minutes are left, so I announce that the room must be cleaned. "Okay," agrees the group.

LEADER'S QUESTIONS

How much history, murder and retribution do the players understand? If they do not understand, do they look upon the story as a mystery to solve? Are they taking the opportunity to solve problems themselves? How does the bird puppet affect the drama?

DAY FOUR

GOALS

- To continue the work, exploring the "brotherhoods" of those on the run and those who must face an important test.
- To use objects and stories as means of persuasion

PLANS

The Potawatomis will be advised by the Great Kinnekinic that they should move their camp to Lamont. In one month there will be another powwow in Lowell with the White Fathers from Washington, D.C. Kinnekinic will urge the families to go to Lowell themselves and consult with the White Fathers. The players will move their camp to Lamont.

The drama as played by the children

At the beginning of this lesson, Meta asks to have her name changed to "Cousin Holiday." No one objects, and it puts her in a good mood for the rest of the drama. The group assembles and shares new treasures. Problems of the village include the move they may have to make. Meta thinks that how to spend the money is an important problem. Traveling Bluebird leaves.

Princess Sunflower distributes more money. She encourages everyone to help in packing. The garden becomes one of the important items to transport. Although it is valuable to the group, the players discover they can run under it, like a parachute, risking ripping it. Everyone has a go at it. The group moves at night. Babies cry. Dogs bark. The load is heavy. But the trip down the river is easy. The tribe finds a quiet place in the forest where they may wait and prepare for their next journey. They plan what to do at the pow wow.

In Lamont, they rest about the campfire, where Traveling Bluebird proves to the villagers that she is indeed Bluebird, giving a blue flower to each person. From an ancient cloth she takes a blue pottery bird, telling the group that it was made by her grandmother at her birth. Although it is covered with dirt, everyone in the group touches it.

"It is beautiful," someone murmurs.

"Shall we go to Lowell to meet the white people, and stand up for our rights? The Big Chiefs in Traverse City say that if we go and make presents for the white people, things will go our way." The group decides to travel to Lowell for the pow wow. "What kinds of presents shall we make?" The players decide on flowers, pictures and treasure necklaces.

Noting the "full moon," Nicole predicts that something will happen. It does. Princess Sunflower sleepwalks through the village. Finally the medicine woman comes with Kinnekinec squawking and flapping.

"Do you villagers have questions? The white men will make demands on you."

"Will they like our gifts?"

"Yes. They will be received with great satisfaction. But you must make some demands on the white man. These demands must be made in writing. Writing is power. That is one of the white man's powers. Who here writes well?" Several hands go up. "I do not write well. How shall I write this?" Princess Sunflower worries.

Kinnekinec cautions, "Begin your writing, 'We Indians want . . .'"

During this, Meta walks in her sleep, wakes up, takes a long pantomimed drink with excellent absorption. She, too, is in some kind of trance. Traveling Bluebird tells the villagers that when she performs as the medicine woman she is in a different world. "I worry that I am crazy," she confesses.

Morning comes. "Everyone wake up."

"Please hold it down, I have a headache still from the trance. It takes so much out of me," the medicine woman moans.

The villagers begin writing. "We Indians want . . . " After ten minutes I read my list. The players are reluctant to read their wants after I have read mine.

The group decides to make a story for the white men. This will be an important gift. Someone says that making stories is boring. I agree that those who do not like to make stories should work on something else. The story is about a beautiful princess who lived in Indiana with her cat. The cat had been kicked in the eye. I ask if losing an eye — being kicked by a horse — may be like losing one's land. Holly, who was the scribe for the story telling, reads the story. (Now even the shyest children are beginning to make substantial contributions to the work.)

It is now time to plan for the final day. I ask the children if they would like to invite their mothers and those who pick them up to a party. There will be a celebration at 2:30 in the afternoon. They decide that it would be good to play games, make presents, and "do some acting" for our guests.

LEADER'S COMMENTS

These sessions were video taped for future classes in theatre at the university. The children were very interested in watching themselves on the tape from the day before. They have no trouble with seeing themselves in role and simultaneously seeing themselves as themselves. Although there was a bit of discussion about the money and who had how much, the conflict went nowhere, as the children were in a very amiable mood. There was possessive behavior over the garden.

Two girls played deeply as they made their bed. Meta performed a complicated pantomimed ritual, grooming herself for the new day. However, in the letter-writing sequence, after I read my letter, the children did not want to share theirs. It closed the possibility of good work for them. Tammy handled this much better by insisting she could not write. I did not not motivate the story-telling well. At this point, I should have let the children decide how they wanted to spend the time. The group needed something more active.

Questions which worked well with the group:

• "Are you ready for the trip?"

• "Did that make Henry a better cat?"

DAY FIVE

GOALS:

• To give the group some dramatic conflict and adventure

• To deal with transportation problems in Michigan in the 1800's

• To explore peaceful confrontation with the enemy

• To explore an Indian celebration in song and dance

PLANS:

The families have prepared for the long journey to Lowell to meet the Great White Fathers from Washington, D.C. They hope for peace and their right to be respected. The journey will be up the Grand, around the Rapids, to a fresh spring, through a swamp, back on the river where the canoe tips over. When the players reach the destination, they will climb up the hill. Pat, a second college student who is joining the group, will be a scout in the U.S. army, spying on the group of Indians as they move to the treaty spot in Lowell.

In Lowell, I will be Senator Gardner; Pat the Senator's assistant, Tate. The players will present gifts, and the requests and resolution. A celebration with popcorn, drinks, an authentic Indian game, fishing and dancing will close the class.

The drama as played

"Perhaps you thought yesterday was a bit quiet. It was. Sometimes life is boring, and it must have been so for the Indians, too. But today I want to take you on an adventure. Because of the activities of the day, there will be certain rules that you must follow. Do you want to go?"

The rules I set out were simple:

• Everyone must believe.
• Everyone must work as a part of the group.
• Everyone must use his imagination.
• You must allow Tammy and me to be several different characters.

I explained that I would play Traveling Bluebird on the way to Lowell, but when the encampment is made, I will become a man, Congressman Gardner. "What is a Congressman?" someone asks. It is hard to believe that these wise nine year olds can have so little information.

I teach the players an authentic toe-heel Indian dance to this prayer —

Wanka, Tonka
Be merciful to me.
We want to live.
That is why we are doing this.

As presents for the Great White Fathers are gathered to be packed, Traveling Bluebird hears bushes rustling. With "Shhh's" the group huddles to make their plans. Pat is spying on us. The spy provides control for the group. Someone spontaneously breaks out into the "Wanka Tonka" prayer.

With treasures, including the rolled-up "garden," the group gets into imaginary canoes. The chant sets the pace for the paddling. At the first campsite, rattlesnakes appear, are speared and eaten for dinner. The group sleeps while someone keeps watch. Nicole and Meta begin to spy on the spy. The whole camp begins to look for Pat, and in the excitement Meta and Nicole are "hurt." Everyone is playing deeply now and finding many adventures. With canoes carried over the heads at a portage, the group encounters difficulty with near drowning and quicksand. Sick people need nursing; someone has lost three fingers on the left hand.

As the group arrives in Lowell there is chaos. Tommy is sick; Princess Sunflower distributes food to all. Major Tate (Pat) dispenses medicine. Nicole makes crutches out of music stands found in the space. Senator Gardner shows a map. All of the land south of the Grand River is now needed by the white men. They will pay for it. The senator is disgusted with all the noise and demands silence from the group. Princess Sunflower reads the requests: "We want our land. We want our animals. We want the land with our fathers' graves. We love our animals. We love peace. We want to live in peace with you. We want to learn about your world. We will teach you about ours. Do not destroy life."

"Show me that you are not savages!" demands the Senator, and then claims, "White people like flowers, trees, kindness. We don't kill. You kill."

"No war," cry the villagers.

"This we do not want, either."

"We want our land. We can get along with you and have peace with you. We have a story to tell you that will show you what good people we are."

Kira reads the story about the Indiana cat. At a slight infraction of behavior, the Senator threatens jail in Ypsilanti. "I wager a pile of money that you don't know singing and dancing!"

"Wanka Tonka," begins Meta. All begin to dance and chant. Major Tate joins in the dance. Gifts are presented, even the vegetables from the garden.

"Now that is valuable!" from the Senator.

Princess Sunflower: "All you think of is money."

"Peace to all," the players cry together as more and more presents are heaped on the table.

"I am rather overcome," gulps Gardner. "More flowers. Absolutely gorgeous. I am ready to sign that treaty. Let us go over the agreements. The trees must be cut down north of the river."

"NO TREES!" in unison.

"We must cut down the trees."

"NO!"

"Everyone must sign. Now, we have south of the river. You have north of the River. Not the Allen's farm."

The players cannot agree if this will be all right, even if it is the first compromise the white people have made.

Noticing the clock, I suggest that everyone take a break from the talks and invite the visitors to the feast. In another day an agreement may be reached. A "Wanka Tonka" dance dedicated to mothers and friends ends the story of the Potawatomis.

LEADER'S COMMENTS ON FINAL LESSON

Children in this lesson were not given enough power. The Indians had all the power taken away from them, and in many lessons the players manifest the behavior of a defeated people.

Although the players may not have learned many facts about Indians and settlers in Michigan, they did have an experience of community and problem solving as they explored drama, pantomime, song, writing, story-telling, and dance.

Controls. Examples of internal control and lack of internal control abound in these lessons. Throughout the lessons I did not talk to the group if they were talking. Having a watchers that was the "enemy" tended to keep a lid on the adventure so that it did not get out of control at the end. All the "shhs" were in role. The dance was taught in a strong leader style of creative drama, where the student follows the teacher. An aspect of control came from the white people being afraid of the Indians because of their history of killing the Allens.

At the beginning the girls fell into their roles more easily than the boys. It is unusual for the boys not to become as deeply engaged as the girls. The fact that girls so outnumbered the boys affected the work. These girls seemed more aggressive and more interested in justice than usual.

Historical accuracy. The prayer/dance was used several times in the adventure. Note how the children use it themselves. This is a good example of the way historiclly accurate elements can be incorporated into a lesson.

Usually I try not to be fussy about physical details, but for believability, I insisted that the canoe seating be in single file. I did not correct the paddling, for I did not think that accurate paddling would be familiar to the majority of children.

Writing and verbal skills. The story written by the group the day before became important in this lesson. However, Princess Sunflower did most of the talking to Senator Gardner. What was the involvement of the children at this time? They had been given the "Mantle of the Expert," but how could I have planned this so that the children had more active power?

Reaching closure. With the rattlesnakes and spy, there was considerable confusion, but the two together tended to heighten the drama. In the sickness scene there was great tenderness. The children enjoyed playing the suffering and didn't want to stop. They were in child time here, but I pulled them on to the conclusion. Was that unnecessary? Since we never reached closure on the treaty, it might have been better to choose working more intently on the illness, a player addition. The suffering looked like chaos. Was it? And did art come out of this chaos? Many times illness was a theme. In a longer session with this same group that tension might bring deeper playing than the themes chosen by the leaders.

COMMENTS ON ENTIRE SERIES OF LESSONS

The leaders often were too strong and did not use questioning well. There were not enough problems posed for the children to solve. The leaders were too anxious to solve the problems for them. Part of this was the result of the children taking some time to get used to the method of work. This could be expected, because building a sense of community cannot be rushed.

It might have been interesting to have let the group decide what kind of a Mrs. Allen I should have been. With the children in on such decisions, belief and satisfaction builds.

The class was too small for many of the usual dynamics of a group of 8 to 10-year olds to take place. This may make the series atypical, but, on the other hand, all drama lessons are atypical.

This class was purely recreational. There was no study component. In the classroom the drama sessions would have had times where the children did research to produce a stronger tie to history.

In using the video tape in this work, I was able to see myself making mistakes that I would never have imagined. I intend to continue to video lessons, because I am sure that monitoring myself will make me a much better drama leader.

Sources

BROWN, DEE. *Bury My Heart at Wounded Knee*. New York: Bantam Books, 1971.

CHAPUT, DONALD. *Michigan Indians*. Hillsdale, MI: Educational Publishers, 1970.

CLASPY, EVERETT. *The Potawatomi Indians of Southwestern Michigan*. Dowagiac, MI: Claspy, 1966.

EDMONDS, R. DAVID. *The Potawatomis: Keepers of the Fire*. Norman, Okla.: University of Oklahoma Press, 1978.

HOFFMAN, CHARLES. *American Indians Sing*. New York: The Joyn Day Co., 1967.

HUIST, CORNELIA STEKETEE. *Indian Sketches*. New York: Longmans, 1912.

LANDES, RUTH. *The Prairie Potawatomis*. Madison, Wis.: University of Wisconsin Press, 1970.

WALTERS, FRANK. *Book of the Hopi*. New York: Ballantine Books, 1963.

HONORING CHARLOTTE

Group: Fifteen third and fourth graders at an elementary school's arts festival

Leader: Laura Gardner Salazar

Time: 50 minutes

Space: Classroom with desks pulled back

Content Goals: To revisit a favorite story, E. B. White's *Charlotte's Web*;

to enter the brotherhoods all who have remembered a departed loved one and all who have planned a large, joyful festival.

Group Goal: To enjoy working together

Drama Goal: To explore character and spectacle

Tensions: These will develop in the group as they work to solve the problems.

Roles: Leader —
Great, Great, Great (etc.) granddaughter of Charlotte, and befuddled organizer of this event

Players—Descendants of Charlotte

Materials: Drawing equipment

I started the lesson with this attention arrestor:

"Well, hello. It is good to see you! Uncle Henry, Hi! (*Shakes hands.*) Aunt Minnie (*a big hug*). And can it be, yes, Charlotte the 15th! And there—there is little Fern and Lurvy. Imagine naming spiders after those kids!

"Well, I know that you are just as curious as can be as to why I invited you here. This is it! At last the American Association of Arachnids have given us, yes, the descendants of Charlotte, the opportunity to have one whole day of their convention to be held in Grand Rapids (*Or whatever city may seem attractive or familiar*) at the Calder.

"Now the tricky part is that we have to put in a proposal to the committee. Do you think that we can plan a day that would be fun for everyone coming to the meeting from all over the world? What has gone over before was a day that was fun, with lots of activities and art work, but this day has to be somewhat serious. After all, our Great Granny Charlotte was a serious being. And Charlotte was an honorable spider! So I am going to ask you first, what do you remember about Charlotte that would make a good celebration?"

After this discussion, the large group broke up into smaller groups who planned an activity that would celebrate something they knew about Charlotte.

The dramatic strategies varied from group to group:

• some groups did scene enactments

• some made tableaux

• some worked in-role

• some did storytelling.

It helped to have the build-in controls of the time constraint, the physical things that needed to be accomplished, and the reference to a beloved story. One group made statues with their bodies, another played "twister," and a third held a spelling contest in Charlotte's honor.

Sources

WHITE, E. B. *Charlotte's Web.* New York: Harpers, 1952.

PRISON AT THE RIVER'S BEND

Group: A kindergarten class at Riverbend School in Grandville, Michigan

Leader: Laura Gardner Salazar, with participation from a class of Grand Valley State University students

Time: Three 40 minute lessons

Space: Intially the classroom, later the gym

Content Goal: To explore the family of all who have cared for another person, and all who have held captives

Group Goal: Concentration

Drama Goal: Plot (expanding upon a simple story)

Roles: Leader — the cook at the prison facility

Kindergarten children — guards

University students — prisoners

DAY ONE

In preparation for this class, I came to the class and met the boys and girls. Later each child, with the help of the teacher, recorded a story on the tape recorder.

DAY TWO

I had listened to the tape and I began by talking to the children about their stories. One that particularly enthralled them was about a talking snowman who had a guitar that was stolen. For a warm-up, the children played the snowman and the guitar thief. The thief, the children said, had to go to jail. They played going to jail, both the jailed and the jailer.

Because kindergarten children want and are given so much structure, it is more difficult using open-ended lessons for their drama work. These children had behaved so well with their teacher that I had assumed that they were very good at following instructions. Was I wrong! In my first day with them, they had no idea how to handle the freedom of a thematic drama lesson. I asked them to go to their tables — they shoved; they pushed; they screamed. When I asked them to do a simple thing, they responded well, but they were rambunctious and full of movement and chatter. When I mentioned that food was needed, they pushed and shoved into the doll corner, even though I had asked them to use only imaginary props.

I knew that it was my fault. I had allowed the children to become overly excited. They had told me of a volatile situation about crime and punishment. The jail experience was exciting. What happened in jail? Bread and water, locked up, escape, running, hitting, violence? There was no connection with sitting and being bored for hours and hours. Information about jail probably came from cartoons. Finally, the time came for me to get back to the university. I ended by telling them that escape from jail is very rare, and if we did a story about prison, there could be no possibility of escape. I told them that at the next session we would play a story about guards and prisoners with my class from the university. I asked them if they would like to be guards or prisoners, and they chose guards.

Somehow I had to get the children back into control, as I expanded their experience of jail. The lesson had to differ from the Saturday cartoons.

DAY THREE

I worked out the following control devices:

- I made name tags that looked like official badges. I would now be able to call children by their names when they wandered away or started running or hitting other children.

- I assigned three child guards to each adult prisoner. If some of them were shy, they would have each other. If they were bold, one of my students should be able to handle three children.

- The work would move to the gym. There would be much more space, yet no chance of children becoming "lost" in part of the room. There were no objects such as the toys in the doll corner to distract or tempt them to use as props.

- I laid out a careful pattern on the floor so that the children could be certain of where they should be at any given time. Each prisoner had a cell about five square feet. There were six cells with an aisle about four feet wide between. The area for the cook (me) was at the end of the aisle, so the cook could see what was going on at all times. The gathering place was between the aisle and the kitchen (the painted tip-up circle on the north side of the gym).

Before the children began, the teacher gave them a "pep talk." I also talked to the children about the necessity to consider what we were doing as work, and not play. I added that there could be no props, no shoving, no running.

The children sat in the black circle, and I told them that everyone would participate, even me. Some of the college students would be in the cells, but did they want the others to be part of the story? "No," they all said. That was fine, and I reminded the kindergartners that the university students not participating would watch.

I knew that I would need some help while I was in role, so I asked Dawn, one of the university students who had shown ease in improvisation, to be the janitor. She was free to move among the children, keeping an eye on problems that might come up. Then I explained that I would turn my back to the group, and when I turned around, the story would begin.

Guards, I have come to talk to you about what has happened. Mr. Brown is nowhere in sight. And this morning I got this letter from him. At least I think it is from him: it's his handwriting.

Dear Cook Salazar:

I have taken sick while visiting California. Please watch over the jail for me. Keep the prisoners healthy and busy.

Mr. Brown, the Warden

How, I asked the children, could we keep the prisoners healthy and busy?

The university students had spent some time segmenting the life of prisoners, and they knew what their needs would be. We had talked about the necessity to be serious and not over-act in the role. They were not allowed to talk to each other, but they could tap on the floor to send signals.

The first thing they asked for was food. The cook distributed the biscuits. One sick prisoner needed help. Two boys said that they knew something about medicine. They examined the prisoner and told the cook that they needed orange juice. Other prisoners asked for reading material, and the cook pointed out a librarian from among the observors, who brought books to the prison. She also pointed out someone who would sell newspapers. Several children told the cook that their prisoner had to go to the bathroom. The cook told them there was a toilet in the cell and the prisoners had to use that.

About seven minutes into the story, as cook I called together the children to see how things were going. They reported a number of problems with the prisoners. They did not like having only biscuits. They wanted other food. Some lesser problems were reported.

The experience for the children was very exciting. They could hardly wait to hear the end of a discussion. They found a lot of the "fun" of the assignment coming from running from the circle to the cells. All of them rushed back to their prisoners to tell them that better food was coming. As cook I made a big pot of spaghetti, and all of the prisoners got some. They asked for other foods such as ice cream, but the cook could not give them such treats.

In the next gathering the children reported new problems. They said that the prisoners wanted to go "outside." With the children's help it was decided that the student watchers could help watch for escapees, and one by one the prisoners could walk around the yard with their guards. This exercise worked well. One prisoner was able to talk her guards into letting her walk around the yard twice.

Next the girls reported that the prisoners wanted to talk to their mothers. A discussion ensued about whether prisoners should be allow to do so. About half the children thought this was not a good idea. They worried that they would escape.

At this point, the drama was getting to an important point. Forty minutes had passed, and the children began to really be in the story. Involvement deepened and problem-solving became important. The children worried that this might be treating the prisoners too well. Others thought that it would be kind to let them see their mothers. The prisoners were seen crying. "What do you think?" one child asked the cook. She answered, "I don't know if it would be right. Mr. Brown said keep them healthy and busy, not happy."

"I think we should," one girl said, and all of the children agreed. At that, out of role, I suggested that each group of guards pick someone from the university student observers to be the mother of their prisoner. This they did with much enthusiasm, and the prisoners and the mothers had a good visit. They hugged and cried.

At the end of this segment the time was up, and one of the college students collected the children for a last time to talk about their experiences. They said that the prisoners were happy to see their mothers, but some of them cried, and some of them asked if they could go home. It made them homesick to see their mothers. They agreed that they would want to see their mothers, too, if they were in jail.

LEADER'S COMMENTS

Not all of the children participated equally. There was still a lot of bumping, running and hitting. The children would have to have much more experience at the drama situation to handle this successfully. Lessons which require moving without touching, and moving in slow motion, would help. The next lesson might all be done without talking. All of these should help to build absorption and a more even involvement.

There was some embarrassment and giggling throughout, but absorption grew. There seemed to be more interest in the mothers' visit than other segments. Despite this, one prisoner did not have any mother visit him at all. The children assigned to him ignored him and found someone more "interesting" to care for. This is not all bad. In fact, it may provide a very interesting piece for the class to work on in future lessons.

Where might this lesson be pursued? Many of the children really were not good jailers. They would throw the food at the prisoners. In a future lesson the prisoners could complain about the treatment that they are receiving, either in or out of role. In many ways the prisoners did have some control over the way they were treated. In later lessons children could play prisoners as well as the guards.

WALK LIKE AN EGYPTIAN

Group: Second and Third Graders at a public museum in a summer course on ancient Egypt working with 10 university students

Leader: Laura Gardner Salazar
A museum teacher

Time: A one-hour class

Space: A large classroom with 2 large tables and chairs off in a corner. The lights were dimmed.

Content Goal: To appreciate the art and culture of the Egyptians

Group Goal: To enjoy our friends and to make new friends

Drama Goal: To explore the way people stood and moved in another period through imitating statues and drawings.

Tensions: Person vs. self

Roles: Leader: Chair of Museum Board

Players: Museum workers

Egyptians

Supplies: Pictures of Egyptian statuary

The lesson started with the students listening to the record of "Walk Like an Egyptian." (A mid-80's recording by the Bangles, SONY Records.)

The leader then drew the students up in group and told them that they could try out walking like real Egyptians. But first they needed to get into the posture of the Egyptians, and the next part of the lesson would help with that.

In the next phase, I called a meeting of all the players:

> "Thank you for coming to this meeting. As the Chair of the Board of the museum, I want to ask you to develop an Egyptian exhibit. We want to make it as much like the real thing as possible."

Out of role I added, "Please get in groups with three of your friends. One of the people in the group will be the statue or picture. Move that person around until you think that he or she is just like the picture you select. The college students will help if you need help. An inspector will be here when you finish, so it must be exact."

The music continued while the players worked. They were very careful to study the pictures. Without talking, they adjusted their partners in the exact posture of the photo.

When the work was complete, the inspector, a university student, walked about making subtle adjustments. I called for several variations, then asked all of the students to assume the pose of the pictures. The music played louder. I told them that now they were animated and they could walk about. They must move very slowly at first to the rhythm of my clapping hands. The statues tried moving to several rhythms.

Now I asked the children if they wished to trade pictures so they could try other poses. All of them but one boy thought that was a good idea. They asked that the college students join in, which they did willingly.

I asked the boy who left the group why he did not want to play. He said he did not like to be a statue. (Did he dislike the touching? Standing still like he was dead?) "Would you be our inspector, then?"

"Yes," he replied solemnly. This was a very quiet class, and he was the most shy student. The boy moved softly among the players, making subtle adjustments.

"The stature are now ready for the exhibit," he announced with deep seriousness.

"Would you like to turn on the motors and give them the rhythm for movement?"

The boy gladly agreed, and using all of his powers of concentration, he switched on the exhibit and clapped out rhythms for the statue's movement until the hour came to an end.

PASSAGE ON "THE ANNE"

Group: 28 sixth graders at Cummings Elementary School

Leaders: Russell Keil, Classroom teacher

Laura Gardner Salazar

Time: Two class periods, one hour each

Space: Large classroom

Content Goal: To understand in more depth the Pilgrim's reasons for coming to the new land.

Group Goal: To make decisions cooperatively and to work together and have fun. Mr. Keil described this class as one that did not especially like each other nor him very well. Part of the problem of working with this class would be to get them to cooperate on any project. They were not hostile to each other, but very independent, and did not gravitate to interaction.

Drama Goal: To dramatize a short story and to understand character motivation.

Tensions: Person vs self

Roles: Leader 1 — Mr. Weston, a merchant who will take the Pilgrims to Plymouth Colony.

Leader 2 — Mistress Brewster, mother of Thomas Brewster, the leader of the English who have emigrated to Leyden, Holland

Students — The Puritans who are considering leaving on "The Anne."

Props: 15 measuring tapes/yard sticks
5 limes
2 rolls of masking tape
Letters — one for every class member

The sixth graders had read a story from their reader, "The First Winter," by Patricia Clapp. This is in the form of a diary and deals with the hardships and death suffered by those who came to New England on "The Mayflower." I used the story as a background to the drama we would create, purposely drawing on the elements of independence, so that students had the option to work alone at first. Later in the lesson there would be cooperative segments. The scenario I developed is based on the problems the Pilgrims still living in Holland encountered after the Mayflower's voyage.

"The Anne" was the second ship to arrive at Plymouth Colony. "The Anne" was 104 feet long and 78 feet at the water line. It was 21 and one half feet wide, providing an average space of six by three feet for each passenger. In the drama many facts about the Mayflower Company and Bradford's group are mingled with inventions to create an interesting story for the sixth graders.

The drama begins at the point where the players have to decide to stay in Holland, return to England, or join their company in the new world.

DAY ONE

THE SITUATION

News comes back to the Puritans living in Holland that those on "The Mayflower" have weathered the first winter. Although news brought from the new world by the fishing fleet out of Plymouth, England indicated that only 50% of the Mayflower Company survived, the English in Holland think that they must sail next summer (1622) on "The Anne." Many of them sent family members and neighbors to found the new colony, and they miss them dreadfully. They must assess their chances to survive in New England. There are nagging doubts that they too will die in their quest for religious freedom. It is the first of November, 1621, Leyden, The Netherlands.

SEQUENCE OF HAPPENINGS

1. Mistress Hannah Brewster speaks to the group, thanking them for the opportunity for a humble woman to take over for her son while he makes preparations for some more of the group to sail on "The Anne."

2. Brewster has a packet of letters with her. These arrive by boat from Plymouth, England and are addressed to those living in Leyden. They came from those who sailed on "The Mayflower" so long ago. Although there have been some rumors and general information brought to the group from various sailing vessels, these are the first personal letters to reach the Puritan band. Mistress Brewster passes out the letters to the group.

My university students had written the letters on a variety of papers, sealing them with wax and scuffing them up a bit. The addresses were to people whose names appeared on the actual manifest of "The Anne," and were signed with the names of survivors of that first winter. Three sample letters follow.

TO SARA RIDER   April, 1621
Dearest Sara,
It seems like forever since we last saw each other. Many times during this last winter my thoughts have drifted to our childhood. The days we spent walking in the fields and dreaming about our futures. Our talks about who we would marry, how many children we would have and other such nonsense. Oh, how my ideas have changed. During the plague last winter I hoped only for life, not worrying about anything else. As you have guessed by my letter,

I have survived and have grown from the experience. Things have begun to brighten up here in the Plymouth Colony. The spring has finally come and the plague is past. The living have gone on with their lives and the people are looking forward to the new life ahead of them. If you decide to come, be prepared; it is very different here than at your father's home.

Your Cousin,
Elizabeth

TO MISTRESS BREWSTER   No Date

Dear Cousin,

This has been the hardest winter I've ever been through. A plague struck and about one third of the people here have died. I know you are considering a voyage across the sea to build a life here. But I feel you should know what has happened.

Death has reached every family and household here. But I feel that the worst is over. Spring is here and those who survived the winter are going to be fine. I only fear what might happen next winter.

If you still plan to come here, you must stay with me.

As always,
Cousin Mary

TO THOMAS MORTON   April 1621

Dear Thomas,

It is spring now, and after a horrible winter, the sun is shining. I can now look ahead to planting the garden.

The boat trip here was a great hardship on everyone. Many people did not survive the trip. Sickness took its toll on almost everyone. Only the strong survived. I must be a survivor. I am sure you too would be a survivor if you decided to come here. We need strong people like you to make our colony work.

I hope you are doing well in your ribbon business in Holland. However, I also hope that you decide to come here. You will be a highly respected member of the colony.

Your old neighbor,
Edward

OTHER WHO SAILED ON "THE ANNE" (This is by no means a complete list, but it is the list of names used in the lesson.)

MEN	WOMEN
William Hilton	Elizabeth Ring
Steve Deane	Mary Singleton
Philippe de le Noye	Priscilla (no last name)
Thomas Prence	Sarah Alerton
Geroge Morton	Patience Brewster
Robert Cushman	Martha Ford
Edward Bompass	Hester Cooke
John Jenny	Sarah Fletcher
William Bassett	Margaret Oldham
John Adams	Elizabeth Warren
Anthony Dix	Mary Glass
Roger Conant	
Experience Mitchell	
Edward Bangs	
Nathaniel Kempton	

Several players read the letter that they received to the class, and in small groups the rest shared the news the letters brought of their relatives and friends in New England. Having the names on the letters automatically gave an identity to the players. The sixth graders were very excited about getting the letters, and Mr. Keil let the rest of the class read their letters aloud later in the day.

Mistress Brewster announces a surprise. Also on the boat from Plymouth was the Londoner, Mr. Thomas Weston, Esquire. Weston had loaned money to those who sailed on "The Mayflower." He now wants to help send "The Anne" to the new world. Weston will help finance the Pilgrims if they pay him back within 10 years. The Puritans will have to pay him 20 English Pounds (about $500.00 in 1987 dollars) for the passage.

Weston is a sharp operator, and looks upon his work with the Puritans as a way to make a lot of money in a short time. History shows him to be a less than nice man.

Weston tells the group that it is a very sound idea to go to Plymouth Colony. Keil, the classroom teacher playing this role is very persuasive. He's playing the villain to the hilt.

At this point, and out of role, I question the group about the part of the story they would like to pursue in the next lesson. The sixth graders have the opportunity to make some choices about the next steps in the drama.

Keil asks the sixth graders to look around the room and to pick one person whom they would trust to lead them if they were in some real danger.

The rest of the hour is used to organize groups made up of people who woud trust each other.

DAY TWO

Group: In addition to the original participants, my class of university students join us for part of this session

To the original **Content** goal and **Group** goal we have added a new **Drama Goal** — Environment and the use of space.

THE SITUATION

The players have decided that they must sail to America. They gather to talk about the practical matters of sailing on such a ship as "The Anne."

SEQUENCE OF HAPPENINGS

Players question Mr. Weston about what worries them. These are the thing they find most worrisome:

> Lack of food
>
> How to store food
>
> Lack of guns
>
> Size of the boat
>
> Crowding
>
> Lack of doctors
>
> Cost

Mr. Weston shows the map of the sleeping quarters. Mistress Brewster suggests that the cabins are very small. The players pick cabin mates for themselves. In groups of four they decide who will be adults and who will be the children and teenagers in the families.

Out of role, I explain how crowded 6 by 3 feet per person is by using a measuring tape and several students. I distribute a tape to each group who then sets up their living space. The college class now enters the drama as the crew of the ship. They help in setting up the space.

- Passengers go to their cabins.

- A storm comes up and everyone gets very sick. The wind howls. The ship tosses in the waves.

- Mistress Brewster insists that everyone must eat a small piece of a lime every day so that they will not develop scurvy. Pieces of real lime are distributed to all. The children playing adults have to figure out how to get the children to eat the sour fruit.

- The ship continues to sail on to America as the story ends.

LEADER'S COMMENTS

The university students who came to the class to observe how drama plays out in the classroom proved to be very useful as bit players. This was one of those lessons that far exceeded the planned goals. Small groups of students cooperated fully. Additional benefits were the fascination with the letters, the cooperation of the students once they saw Mr. Keil get into role, and the quiet joy the players expressed through the lesson.

Sources

CLAPP, PATRICIA. "The First Winter," *Measure Me Sky.* Lexington, MA: Ginn and Company, 1976, pp. 333-347.

IN THE LAND OF THE KISH

Group: 26 sixth graders at the Maplewood Elementary School, Jenison, Michigan, working with 35 university students in Theatre for Children

Leaders: Gloria VanWestenbrugge, classroom teacher
Laura Gardner Salazar

Time: One day a week for six weeks every Friday morning in connection with student's social science unit on the beginnings of Western Culture.

Space: School gymnasium

Content Goal: To better understand the life of early peoples.

To understand the problems of being a slave.

To appreciate functions of language.

Group Goal: To enjoy working together and working with adults as equals

Drama Goal: To explore the interior life of a character

Tensions: A powerful group vs a weak group of people

Roles: Van Westenbrugge — The Princess of the defeated and enslaved Damascans

Salazar — Weak Old Queen of the Kish

6th Graders — People of the Kish

University Women Students — Enslaved Damascans

University Men Students — Kish ministers

The entire set of lessons from these classes were not documented, but the instructions to the participants clearly outline the possibility of the incidents which followed.

INSTRUCTIONS TO THE WOMEN OF THE UNIVERSITY CLASS

- You are prisoner/slaves captured and brought back to the Kish after a war in which your people attacked the Kish.

- The men from your land, Damascus, were killed in the fighting. Your children have died of a plague. You may be young, middle-aged, or old; sick, or healthy. You are very sad.

- You do not speak the language of the Kish people.

- You will be assigned as a personal slave of a student-family group.

- They will set you to work making bricks.

- You have not made bricks before. You do not like it.

- You have a written language and you try to keep records of how you are being treated. There is only the ground to write on. You need a stick or bone or something to make markings. Do not let the Kish people see you writing, for they do not know how to do this, and you do not want to give them your power. Your Queen is Mrs. VanWestenbrugge.

INSTRUCTIONS TO MEN OF THE UNIVERSITY CLASS
(There were three.)

- You are ministers of the land of the Kish. Your people will be spending the great riches they have taken from the Damascan women to build a beautiful new city for their pleasure.

- Friday I will send them in groups to instruct the stupid slaves on how to make bricks. While the slaves work on this project, the Kish people will draw the plans for their palaces, gardens, temples, and market places.

The content of many of the lessons dealt with the people of Kish's struggle to teach the slaves how to make bricks and how to speak the Kish language (gibberish). The captors came to like their slaves and to relate to them.

The old queen seemed treacherous. The Kish and Damascans whispered together about her evil ways and how she favored her ministers, rough and harsh taskmasters. Was the Old Queen trying to steal the power from her absent son? At this point, the Princess of the Damascans led a revolt of her enslaved peoples. As a group, they agreed to throw off the old Queen and to join the Kish in developing a new nation and culture. The Kish tried the Old Queen and sent her to jail, and the new peoples celebrated.

RUN DMC

Group: 32 junior high school students visiting Grand Valley State University to participate in the King-Parks-Chavez program

Leader: Laura Gardner Salazar

Time: 2 sessions, The first was 2 hours, the second 4 hours

Space: School of Communications video studio

Content Goal: Honoring ethnic heroes (Social Science)

Group Goal: To define a goal and cooperate with each other to reach it.

Drama Goal: To explore character. To polish technical aspects of a presentation.

Tensions: Individual vs Loved ones

Roles: Leader — Did not take a role

Players — Rap Star Run DMC

Important people in his life

The King-Parks-Chavez program at Grand Valley State University was developed to give talented minority junior high school students, who might never consider going to college, a successful experience in a college setting. The School of Communications at GVSU developed an experience for these young people where they would have the chance to prepare some material for a television presentation. Students were broken into three groups. One group worked as "talent" in a drama, another ran cameras and sound, and the third worked as editors in the control booth. In alternating sequence, each group had a chance to perform each function. Six classes went through the process each year. The subject for each session was different, but heroes often were explored.

The first day the method of working was introduced, and on the second day students were asked to pick their hero and develop scenes and tableaux from his or her life.

One class seemed to be particularly difficult the first day. They gave only surface attention, and the boys in the group appeared much too mature for the material I had picked for demonstration. Truthfully, I did not look forward to the second day when I would work with their hero.

When that morning arrived, the class seemed to be ready to test me, but I was ready to challenge them. Other groups had chosen to work with the life of Rosa Parks and Harriet Taubman. I was expecting to have the group give me the name of some equally prominent African American hero. But the group had planned no person to study. Their chaperones had not heard that I had given an assignment.

I asked for several suggestions. These were slow in coming, but eventually we had some names on the board. Finally one tall boy in the back said, "Run DMC." I had never heard of this rap star, and didn't know how to write his name on the board. The group thought that this was very funny, but I became curious. Who was this person? Was this a group? Each question elicited laughter, but the players were clearly in the expert position. They enjoyed the fact that they knew more than the college professor. They took a vote and Run as their hero.

"Can you be serious if we choose a rap star to be our hero?" I asked.

"Oh, yes, yes!"

"Then tell me some things about Run." I said. And we were off, attempting to understand the life of a rap star.

Some of the categories we segmented as we looked at a powerful and rich person's life were

> friends
> talents
> school
> family
> handling money
> privacy
> religion

The players decided to do four scenes from the life of Run. The three students who had been the most restless on the first day composed a rap that they delivered as the narrative for the scenes as they were videotaped.

- The first scene was in Heaven where the angels gave the about-to-be-born Run gifts which would serve him well here on earth: the gift of a fine voice, the gift of "scratch," the gift to be black.

- The second scene took place as Run was exploring what it was to have one family member gifted, while the others were ordinary people.

- The third scene took place in Run's church where the preacher delivered a sermon on the evils of rap.

- In the fourth and final scene, many relatives and hangers-on came to Run's door and begged for money from the star.

LEADERS COMMENTS:

The students were perfectly concentrated. They worked very hard to make the scenes realistic and meaningful. They came to trust me and I came to trust them. The result was far more interesting and artistic than the drama developed from the heroes the teachers had chosen in the past. I would not usually recommend such a complex project for a four-hour time frame, but it stretched the students to their ultimate best, and they succeeded to everyone's satisfaction.

INDIAN SALT BELONGS TO INDIA

A Drama Lesson on Peace Based on the Life of Gandhi

Group: Ten players aged 13 through 18 at a city-wide church peace celebration. Some players came with friends, but the whole group did not know each other. The number of players could be anywhere from 7 to 30 players.

Time: 90 minutes. The lesson might be more effective if played over 3 hours and taught on separate days.

Space: Open room

Content Goal: To understand what it means to stand up for what is right without resorting to violence.

Group Goal: To have an interesting time together.

Drama Goal: To explore character.

Tensions: Indians vs the British

Players vs themselves

Roles: Leader — In 1930's episode, Gandhi's Wife, Kasturbai Gandhi

In 2030's episode, Ms. Shipley, an assistant museum director for the National Peace Museum and Head of the American exhibits

Players — In 1930's episode, friends of those who are going with Gandhi. Later those who are activists themselves. Some may also play westerners who have come to observe Gandhi's work.

In 2030 episode, designers and the Board of Directors for the National Peace Museum, including the President of the Board, monument designers, diagram designers, Editor of the "Peace News," representatives of other media, fund raisers, directors of the Smithsonian Museum, and others as needed.

Materials: Writing paper
Pencils
Letters from Gandhi and those on the march
Polaroid camera and film
Video tapc: Vol. 2 of the Richard Attenborough movie, *Gandhi,* starring Ben Kingsley, including the segments on march to the sea and Indians making their own salt.

Basis of Lesson:

The lesson was based on this paragraph from the autobiography of Mohandas K. Gandhi:

> "The salt tax was extremely unpopular and a powerful movement had been for some time past going on to secure its repeal. I therefore suggested that the people might prepare salt from sea-water in their own houses in disregard of the salt law."

THE LESSON
PART ONE: MOTIVATION

Leader: "Today we will be using drama to explore one of the most interesting times of the Twentieth Century. You will be transported to a different time and a different land, but you will keep your own personality if you like. You may participate actively or less actively. The only rules that we will use are not to disrupt except in the context of the drama. I am asking you for the game's sake to believe the big lie. I think that you will catch on as we go along, so let's move into the drama as fast as we can. One last word, I will use the word "curtain" to stop and start the drama. Now I am going to go off, and when I come back the drama will have begun."

(Leader goes off, turns her back and in about 20 seconds returns to the group. Visibly upset, she says something like the following.)

"I suppose you heard the latest about Gandhi. Oh, I am so worried about him. You know what a man he is for ideas. Such a good man. A saint. The only lie he ever committed was that he never told his parents that he at one time ate meat. They went to their cremations not knowing.

"Of course, I know that he is brilliant, but he will not listen to me. You know the British have their guns and they are not afraid to use them. . .

"Just think of the cruelties that the British have perpetuated right here in this village. I know that today your brother (*pointing at one of the boys*) is languishing in jail in Calcutta for publishing the "Free India" newspaper. I know that your (*pointing to a girl*) father was killed in the Great Massacre at Amritsar along with your sister and her baby! And are there other injustices that I do not know? (*Players will add as they wish.*)

"Well, Gandhi's latest idea is that Indians must make their own salt. I do not understand it. He has written this letter so that you will understand. Please can someone read? I suppose you know that I read only with great difficulty. Women do not read. As a little girl I was not allowed, and then by the time Gandhi tried to show me, it was so hard."

Someone reads the letter. Discussion may follow.

> "As I have told you, there is no word directly from Gandhi, but we have been sent some film that I want you to see. I have looked at it, and I thought I needed your advice on what to do next.

Show part of the tape of the movie on the march to the sea.

PART TWO: A DECISION TO JOIN GANDHI

This may or may not be in role. There is no need to strictly adhere to role at this point.

Leader: What shall we do?
Shall we select a leader?
Should I continue to lead?
Would you like to have some specific roles in the enactment?
Would you like to have a leadership role?
Shall we join Gandhi now?
Shall we stay here and await the news?

The group votes on whether to join Gandhi or stay and wait for the news. If they can not decide, they could explore both possibilities. If they decide to wait, they will follow the first set of directions; if they choose to join the march, they will do the second set of activities outlined below.

STAY AND WAIT

- What are your hopes for India?

- Show us what you want for yourself and family.

- Break into groups and plan tableaux of your hopes.

- Show the results to each other.

- What are your fears for your loved ones?

- Write a letter to someone that you love who is going on the march with Gandhi.

JOIN THE MARCH

- Make tableaux of the march. In groups show:

    Happy Marchers

    Happy crowds

    A hard time

- Show a tableaux of fellowship in the evening.

- Write a letter to someone you love.

PART THREE: AT THE SEA

Leader: "I can wait no longer. Let us go to the sea and make salt. I will depend upon you to lead the salt-making (*pointing to one boy*). I call upon you to head up the salt selling (*pointing to one girl*). I see that three foreign journalists have joined us. Let us show them how we work in India."

In role everyone becomes makers, buyers and sellers of salt or foreign journalists. The journalists arrive to interview and photo the workers. They take Polaroid pictures of the work.

PART FOUR: PASSIVE RESISTANCE

Leader: (*out of role*) "Now let us go back and see the news reel of the next development."

- See videotape from movie of salt selling scene and resulting violence at the seaside.

- Letters arrive from friends and relatives who were at the sea. Some of the letters are for the players. They read them. See sample letters at the end.

- Discussion, as they share information from the letters.

    Was it hard to not fight back?

    Was it worth it not to fight back?

    What was gained?

- Players pose for photographer showing the brutality at the salt mine.

Show section of the video tape that reveals that Gandhi has convinced the British that they can not win in this instance.

PART FIVE: REMEMBERING A HERO

Leader: (*Out of role*) "The year is 2030. The Great Peace Museum in Washington D.C., which was founded in 2010, the year that nuclear weapons at last were dismantled, is expanding. It is opening a Gandhi wing to celebrate the wisdom of this great leader who taught us how to achieve justice without violence."

Leader: (*As Museum Associate, Mrs. Shipley*) "Thank you for coming to this first meeting of the Gandhi Memorial Wing Committee. I'd like to have you get acquainted with each other.

Various players are assigned roles by the leader saying such things as: "Mr. Brown, this is David Jones, the editor of "Peace in Our Times."

"Now let us turn our attention to the business at hand. How can the Peace Museum honor Gandhi? What would be appropriate and tasteful? What would make it easy for people to understand this complicated time in which he lived?"

A board meeting follows in which the members discuss ideas on how to honor Gandhi. Mrs. Shipley asks the group to break into pairs where they begin to plan the work for the museum. These are some activities that could take place.

• Draw plans for the Gandhi wing.

• Show us through tableaux how the exhibits will look.

• Create materials for the exhibits.

• "Film a movie" on the most important moments from Gandhi's life.

• Plan a statue for the lawn of the museum.

The group shares these ideas and enactments for as long as there is interest. This may prove to be the longest and most exciting part of the lesson. It must be open ended, however, to provide time for remembering incidents from the four parts above.

It may be appropriate for the whole lesson to end in a celebration.

LEADER'S COMMENTS: I found it important to not over-plan this lesson. There is the danger of the teacher becoming inflexible if some parts are not left to improvisation. With the holes in the lesson, the leader sincerely looks to the students to help solve the problems the situation presents. She becomes an explorer into the content along with the youth. In the event that the leader is a man, this could be a colleague or other relative of Gandhi.

Evaluation time was built into the lesson through the photos, letters and discussion.

SAMPLE LETTERS

If possible, have the letters addressed to particular people. They should be written in different hands and with a variety of paper and envelopes. Some names and dates are fictitious. Feel free to change these as meets the needs of the group.

Parbandar, India
June 3, 1930

My Dear Friends:

My beloved wife, Kasturbai, has asked me to write this letter to explain in my own words why we are going to march to the sea. That way she will be free to add what she knows without contradicting me.

The salt tax is very hard on all Indians, but especially those who are very poor. In this hot land, little can stay fresh without salt. The British have taken a monopoly on the salt and we must buy it from them with a very high tax.

But Indian salt must be for India. We have all the salt we need right here in the ocean. We do not have to buy it from the British.

Therefore I propose to march 240 miles to the sea and to make salt. We will sell it there at a fair price, and the British will have to make do. Remember how the American colonies opposed the tea tax? They did something about it, they threw it into the Boston harbor. But alas, they then took up arms and reverted to violence. We will not do so.

Send us your prayers on our journey.

Your Humble Servant, Gandhi

To Sheth Ambalal
July 23, 1930

Dear Cousin,

I send a hasty note. We know that you will have read about the incident at the ocean. Gandhi did not allow us to fight back, yet we were brave. Will you join us?

Umar Sabani

To Miss Anita Syngh
July 31, 1930

Dear Miss Syngh:

I am very sorry to inform you that your brother Rajid received a serious head injury in the salt incident last week. The doctor says that he may not live much longer. Can you come?

Sincerely yours,

Siraj Plassey

To Masime Malaviyaji
July 29, 1930

My dear Wife,

Life here has been very hard. Many were injured. But we will not give up. Some wives are selling the salt. But you must stay away. I love you and our baby, but I must follow Gandhi on his quest for justice.

Your loving husband
Sivaji Villabhbhai

To Shirmati Naidu
July 30, 1930

Dear Shirmati,

Will you forgive me? At last I have come to my senses. I have deserted His Majesty's Army and have joined Gandhi's resistance movement.

Do not try to find me. I am going into hiding.

Your friend,
Vithal das Jerajani

To Margaret Bourke-White
July 29, 1930

Dear Miss Bourke-White:

Thank you for the copies of the articles in LIFE MAGAZINE. Your continued interest in our work is greatly appreciated. Wish us success in our march to the sea and the salt making with the water of the Indian Ocean. India's salt must be for Indians.

Your Humble Servant,
Mohandas K. Gandhi

To Urmile Devi
July 30, 1930

Dear Friend,

The attack of the troops of the Empire was devastation. Gandhi asked us if we were strong enough to face the soldiers with guns and to a man we said, "Yes!" I wish I could tell you how easy it was to not fight back. It was not easy, and I was tempted to fight back. I am so ashamed that I made a fist and that our friend Pandu Nehru had to stop me. I must work harder to control my temper.

Yours, Jahangir

Source

GANDHI, MAHATMA. *Mahatma Ghandi, His Own Story.* New York: Macmillan, 1930.

OREGON OR BUST

To get this series of lessons going, I prepared the following handbills:

WOMEN
OPPORTUNITY IN OREGON
OREGON MEN NEED WIVES!! FREE TRIP TO OREGON
MEET MR. GATREAU AT THE IMPERIAL HOTEL
WELL CHAPERONED   REFERENCES REQUIRED
APRIL 15, 1857   MUST HAVE $50.00 CASH

Group: 37 university students, almost all in teacher training programs

Leader: Laura Gardner Salazar

Time: Four class periods of three hours each

Space: The classroom and, in the 4th session, the theatre with its catwalk above the stage

Content Goal: To introduce college students to the thematic method of teaching drama

Group Goal: To get the group to commit to drama work physically as well as verbally

Drama Goal: To understand a large sweeping epic

To play a character far from self

Tensions: Woman vs. nature

A group of "little" people vs. one powerful person

Roles: Students —35 single women of marriageable age going to Oregon; 2 wagon masters

Leader —Mistress Anne Smith, widow of a wealthy New England sea captain, and sister of Elias J. Howe, the man who organized this expedition. She will serve as chaperone. She has never been west of the Green Mountains before.

Equipment: For the first few lessons, pencils, pens, paper and note cards.

For the final class, dishes, mirrors and other trinkets from the prop room that looked as though they might be of value. Some were broken or chipped. A bag of scraps and some quilt pieces.

Preparation:

Before starting the series I told the class

It is 1857. You are going west to Oregon. The men there need wives, and they are willing to pay for your trip out there. You must take enough money, $50.00, to make the trip home, in case you do not want to stay Think about these things:

> Why are you going to Oregon?
> How old are you?
> Have you been married before?
> Are you in good health?
> Do you have children?
> What do your parents think about your going?
> Why do you think you are suited to the work on the frontier?
> Do you know how to shoot a gun?

Go to the library and find out some facts about life at this time; about the education of a woman aged 20 to 30; about women's legal rights at this time. What food would you take on such a journey? What would clothes be like? What furniture and treasures would you take along? What was the Oregon Trail like?

DAY ONE
"On Being a Spinster in 1958"

The women got into groups of 4 or 5 and talked about their research, and reported back to the central group. Meanwhile the wagon masters planned how they would interview the women who proposed to go to Oregon.

The wagon masters passed out the handbills, and the women talked informally about what they wanted to ask the wagonmasters.

The women went to the hotel and wrote to a family member about their hopes and fears. This exercise was the most valuable part of getting into character, they said later.

.They came down to the hotel lobby and found other women being interviewed, strolling about the premises, talking in small groups and getting acquainted.

SAMPLE LETTERS

St. Louis, Missouri.
March 20, 1857

To Poplar Bluffs, Missouri

My Dearest Sarah,

I arrived in St. Louis yesterday. It was a dull journey. But my arrival here was very exciting. I have never been in such a large town.

I miss you and David dearly, but I feel that I must get on with my life. A new beginning is just what I need to dull some of my memories.

There are many women here that want to go on the trip to Oregon. I only hope that I will be selected to make the journey. I look forward to starting a new life in another place, even though the unknown can sometimes be terrifying.

I want to thank you and David so much for providing references for my trip. If you see Rev. Brown, please express my gratitude to him, also. I am sure that these letters will help me gain a spot on the wagon train.

I will write again when I next get the chance.

Gratefully yours,
Your Friend, Helen

Dear Ma.

I just got here. The Hotel is 10 of our barns put together. I'm suppose to go down in a few minets to meet these people who are in charge.

I hope they know what there doing. Iv seen some of the other women. Don't look like none have ever lifted a finger.

I have a feeling this trip is goner be a hard one. These little Prisies arent gona make it. Im strong enough. You and Pa taught me how to work.

I wonder what the mountains look like. I here theys bigger than ars. I cant amagen anything that big. I know how hard it is cross the Apps.

Well, I hope everything will work out for us. I'll write when I can.

Love, Marci

March 8, 1857

Paddy O'Reilly
Dublin, Ireland

My dear brother Paddy,

Trust you and Colleen and the babies are well.

I have left the Kennedys in Boston and am now in St. Louis to leave soon for Oregon Territory to get me a husband.

I am not afraid to travel. It cannot be worse than the boat ride to America from Ireland.

You know I am used to hard work as a maid and before that on the farm. This is a chance for a new life and maybe even some wee ones for me.

God bless you,
Bridget
P.S. Fr. Mulroney wrote this for me.

DAY TWO
"Signing up for the Trip"

As the class entered the room, I handed each student a card with a suggestion about character on it. Some of them were

- Tell a lie about your character to five select people. Tell them it is a secret. Deny it when others ask about it.
- Gossip about someone you have met since you came to the hotel.
- Tell a secret about Mrs. Smith's family back in Salem, Massachusetts.
- Brag about your family.

Mrs. Smith held a reception for the women going on the train. Tea was served and the women chat about their backgrounds and what the future may hold for them. At the same time, the men in the class began interviewing to see if they will be acceptable for the trip. I passed the following form for them to fill out, and asked the women to give assistance to those who could not read and write.

Preliminary Interview

Name:
Residence:
Marital Status: Health:
Dependents (Names and Ages):
Father's Name:
Name of Closest Living Male Relative:
Religion:
References (3):
Reasons for Change of Status:
Signature: Date:

I wanted the women to feel the constraints of being a foreign woman in a homogeneous, sexist and prudish society in the 1800's as often as possible. I also asked each woman to limit her possissions to two hundred pounds. She had to submit a list of them. Mrs. Smith submitted the following: 2 boxes of china; 1 chest of bedding; I chest of clothing; Great Grandma Kinne's walnut chest; 1 box of cooking utensils; I box misc; 1 rifle.

Committing these ideas and items to paper further helped the women to discover who they were. At this point the interviews were held, and those who were going to go on the trip were announced. One woman was not permitted to go because she had young children. Mrs. Smith later smuggled her and her children on her wagon. When they were discovered, in a later lesson, the group had to decide how to handle it.

At the end of the lesson the group spent time segmenting the possible needs of the women. They came up with the following list:

The physical move itself
Food
Safety
Interpersonal relations
Laws
Sleeping
Medicine

The group chose to work on the physical move itself and interpersonal relations. They also discussed the brotherhoods that had so far been explore. The women identified

All who are chosen/not chosen
All who wait
All who hope for the future
All who face the unknown.

The men added

All who test
All who lead
All who are responsible for others.

DAY THREE
"Disease in the Cattle"

The wagon master was not in class this day, so I had to improvise a lesson. In the role of Mrs. Smith, very sadly and seriously I presented the group with the problem that three oxen had died of a mysterious disease. It was the first time deep emotion had been tried with the group, and Mrs. Smith cried as she told the women that Mr. Gautreau had gone to Iowa to try to purchase some more. Everyone, she said, would have to chip in part of their $50.00 to replace the dead oxen. There was much resistance to this, and the group began to suspect that Mrs. Smith was trying to get more money. Others defended her. Rumors about Mrs. Smith, started at the last meeting, continued. Neither Mrs. Smith nor I knew, until the end of the lesson, that the rumor had to do with her drinking problem!

We discussed possible solutions for the problems with the cattle — everything from doubling up in the wagons to leaving some belongings behind or having a lottery to eliminate some of the women.

DAY FOUR
"The Wheel off the Wagon"

At this point in the group's work, I thought it was time for a real "adventure," rather than more talk. It is hard to give grown women this kind of adventure in a classroom. Then I thought about the excitement of all the students I know when they are taken up to the metal catwalk above the auditorium and stage. With its solid railings it is very safe, yet takes the breath away on first encounter. This could be a genuine adventure that is safe.

134

I took the dishes and trinkets and laid them carefully along the catwalk and up the circular stairs to the catwalk. I wrote the name of each item on a piece of paper. There were not as many items as there were pieces of paper, so that some people would not find their valuable possessions.

At the beginning of the class I entered as Mrs. Smith, and told the group that there had been an accident with the supply wagon at the last river crossing. The wagon had lost a wheel, and all of the supplies tumbled out. On the bank about half a mile downstream there were some items that might belong to the group.

I pulled the pieces of paper out that listed the "valuables." They gave the name, the item, and value. Helen Richardson's blue willow plate was listed as having "sentimental" value. Virginia Westcott had packed a red velvet-covered box valued at $20.00. There was a Family Bible, a silver chalice, a kerosene lamp. I said these were the items people had packed in the extra wagon. Who owned the silver tray? Whose was the blue willow plate? etc.

I announced that I would take groups of five to the site of the accident to search for the missing pieces. I asked the rest of the group to make camp, and to teach the younger girls quilting. One student asked if she could go down to the creek and hunt for those deer that had been seen there. She led a hunting party who eventually cleaned the deer and cooked it. The men in the class were stationed in the light booth, the entrance to the catwalk, where they worked on fashioning a new wheel for the wagon.

The list of possessions was treated as if it named more than "made up" items. The group fell into belief as they claimed each item. I could not remember who had what name in the story, so I could not give the possessions to particular people. Therefore I depended on the class to claim each item. It was an exciting moment, providing an interesting controversy when two people said they both owned the same silver plate.

At this juncture half of the students were handed slips of empty paper which made them soldiers at the fort. Music was put on the phonograph and cider and doughnuts completed the party. Mrs. Smith taught everyone the Virginia Reel, and the women had their worst suspicions confirmed. Mrs. Smith did get tipsy. Daisy was found with her two children in Mrs. Smith's wagon.

The drama now took on a life of its own, and little planning was needed on my part to maintain dramatic tension. Just at this point the drama had to end because the class was drawing to a close. We found no time later in the term to return to the work, except for twenty minutes one day when the class "returned to Oregon for a centennial of the women's trek." Everyone was asked to imagine "going to the library" in the town and finding out what happened to their character. The class did the activity half-heartedly.

Clearly this was not the lesson that they wanted. They wanted to meet those men!

LEADER'S COMMENTS

Some of the students were concerned that the last lesson about the sick oxen was not finished. Participants needed to say that they wanted to know about the oxen. I had not pursued the oxen story, because I thought that it could not provide the adventure and fun the group needed at that point The group was losing interest, and it needed to have a good time more than it needed continuity. Group goals took precedence. With drama we can skip about. When I asked the class if they wanted to know what happened to the oxen, all agreed that they wanted to know, but did not want to work it out.

There was a problem in taking small groups off (as I did on the "wagon wheel" day) and expecting the large group to go on its own. The hunting, cooking, fuel gathering and quilting did not go well. Having a second leader would have helped here.

This class was almost too cooperative. They were not in the least rebellious, but some of them did begin to enjoy risking their reputations for perfection and came to play hookers and criminals.

They wanted the class to end with a big party where they could meet their future husbands. Had the class not been my only group that summer, I might have "hired" male students from other classes to fulfill their fantasies.

THE HOUSE OF CHRISTINE

Group: Thirty-five future drama leaders in summer school.

Leader: Laura Gardner Salazar

Time: 3 hours spread over three days

Space: The stage of the university theatre

Content Goal: To explore the aspects of high-pressured business.

Group Goals: To empower the group. Often I find the classes I teach composed of women who have little confidence in their lives. Most of them relish an opportunity to view themselves in a powerful but feminine way to discover ways to bring new people into the group, and at the same time to criticize them constructively.

Drama Goal: To develop character in very different circumstances than the players' own.

Tensions: Woman vs. Woman

Woman vs. Nature (time)

Roles: Leader — Mlle. DuBois and Christine (never appeared, only communicated through writing)

Players —Designers and other workers at "The House of Christine"

DAY ONE

On the first day of the drama I arrived in the classroom breathlessly. I greeted the group using a "phony" French accent. Then I announced that a telex had arrived for the company, and I would read it to everyone.

To: The Grand Design Group

From: Christine

Re: Spring 1990 Clothing

Pardon this curt memo, but as you'may know, I have been ordered by my doctor to spend 6 weeks relaxing completely after collapsing in New York last week. I have chosen a quiet village in the Swiss Alps, where I will take long walks and try to forget the pressures of creating a world-class house of fashion in a small midwestern city.

But, my dears, you will be in my mind every waking moment. In my absence, I have sent my friend and respected colleague, Jeannine DuBois, who will look over my interests well. I am sure you know that Jeannine has been with Yves St. Laurent in Paris and Houston.

Please look after her. She has promised to run the design department democratically, and I hope that she will inspire you to do your best. She also will keep an eye on the books. Mlle. DuBois will call me every day to report your progress on the spring line.

One thing that continues to bother me is that we have so many new people in the design department this summer. Please do everything that you can to integrate them into your projects. We must stand together at this time.

But on to more positive things—When I arrive back in Grand Rapids in September, I expect to see a line of clothing that will set New York and Paris on their ears! Remember the reputation we have established over the last 20 years!

Mme. Christine

Out of character, I asked the class to get into seven groups of five each. In addition, I asked eight players to draw a card. Each card had one of the following written on it:

"You are new to the group. You are a former model with another firm."

"You are new to the group. You just graduated from the Kendall School of Design."

"You are new to the group. You just graduated from the Paris, France Design Institute."

"You are a former model with this firm. You have just

started to design."

"You are new to the firm. You are an ex-movie star learning the business."

"You have been with the firm all 20 years it has been in existence."

"You have just been promoted to the design group from the secretarial pool You came to the company when you were 17. Now you are 34."

"You consider yourself to be underpaid."

As DuBois, I then challenged the group to come up with some designs that would capture the attention of the design world. She told them that everything had to be new. New fabrics, new lines, new colors. Each group was assigned one of the following: Rain wear, accessories, evening dresses, sports clothes, office wear, lingerie, and beach wear. The seven groups worked together to develop some ideas for their designs.

DAY TWO

The second day, still in the role of Mlle DuBois, I brought in a bundle which I announced was the grandchild of Mme. Christine. The players were encouraged to hold the "baby" and to talk about the future of the design house. They speculated that the baby would have a future in fashions, and talked about what gifts the child would need to become successful in her own right.

DAY THREE

On the third day, the class made formal presentations of their designs. As each group presented their drawings, other students passionately scrutinized them. Players worked very hard to convince the group that their ideas were the best. Finally a line was adapted, and a celebration concluded the series of lessons.

NOTES:

The time this class had to work was shortened by outside circumstances, and DuBois' phoney accent was never exposed, nor were all of the new people integrated into the larger group.

In a variation on this lesson, another class made elaborate plans for a fashion show. The day before the big event, a fatal communicative disease developed among the workers. The players had to decide whether to continue their public show or to cancel it indefinitely. They also worked on the problems of discovering how people were being infected, and how to avoid a multimillion dollar lawsuit.

OLD CHARLEY

Group: Detroit inner city Senior High School drama class that had been studying heroes

Leader: Laura Gardner Salazar

Classroom Teacher

Time: One class period

Space: Drama classroom

Content Goal: To appreciate others

Group Goal: To cooperate in improvisation

Drama Goal: To explore heroes, to build dramas from student's stories

Tensions: The hero struggling with himself

Roles: Leader 1 — Waiter

Class: Other characters in the story

A high school student in an inner city shared this story with the drama class:

> "Two years ago I ran away from home. My mother and I live together in a small place, and she never cared for me. She does crack. She didn't do nothing for me. I got tired of it. I thought I was grown, so I got out on the street.
>
> "Man, I didn't know anything. I was so dumb I didn't know where to sleep or where to eat. The street wasn't no place for a thirteen year old kid, but I thought I was grown.
>
> "In about two weeks the police picked me up and put me in a detention house. I was there for nine months. Now I can't believe that I was so dumb to think I could make it on the streets.
>
> "I wouldn't ever do that again, but it's hard when your mother doesn't care for you." *The storyteller spoke softly with genuine tears in his voice.*

"Has anything like that happened to the rest of you?" I wasn't sure that the story was true, and didn't want to be led on. Several other students said that they had been runaways. "Would you like to work on a story based on this idea?" The group agreed that this would be interesting. It no longer mattered if the story was true of not; the class was ready to work. What follows is a transcription of the lesson.

"Put the chairs together like this," I said as I arranged four desk/chairs facing each other. "Think for a minute. You are at the local place to go to get a snack. I will motion you to come into the story two at a time and give you an idea who you are."

In the role of a waiter at Jerry's Restaurant, I asked couples if they knew what had happened to Jimmy. At this point I did not know, either.

Waiter:	They say he's run away. Have you seen him? Have you talked to him? Shhh! We have to keep this quiet. I'm worried sick. And his mom was in here before. (*Between talking and delivering orders, the waiter heard this information.*)
Student 1:	Nobody's seen him for two days.
Student 2:	Lediane was with him at the park.
Student 3:	His old car is still parked in front of his house.
Student 4:	Someone saw him down by the river.
Waiter:	Shhh! (*Interrupting*) Who's this? I thought it was. It's Jimmy's mother and her new boyfriend. Don't talk to them. Jimmy wouldn't want us to.
Leader 2:	(*As Jimmy's Mother*) Hi. I'll have a grilled cheese and a Pepsi. (*Pause.*) To go. (*Pause*) Hi, Latricia. Hi Tyrone. What are you looking at? You know Jimmy isn't at home! You probably know just where he is and I am sick! Sick I tell you. You'd better tell me if you know.
Tyrone:	We don't know, Mrs. Cook. We haven't seen him since he was with Lediane at the park. . . (*Pause*) two days ago.
Leader 2:	Well, I'm taking my order and leaving, but if I find out one of you is hiding my Jimmy, you will hear it from me! (*She stomps out.*)
Waiter:	What does she think she's doing, never cared for him when he was with her.
Tyrone:	You know, I bet he could be down near the river. Sometimes he goes there.
Dewaine:	You know that old guy, Charley. That weird old guy. He has a fishing shack down at the river. Sometimes Jimmy talks about going down there to see him.
Latricia:	I'd be afraid to go see Old Charley. He's weird. He smells. He talks funny, and he is so old, he's ready to die!
Student 1:	Some people say he's crazy and should be locked up!
Waiter:	Well, we could go down there and sort of scout around. We wouldn't have to talk to anyone.

At this point, I stopped the action to discuss what happened. "Are you happy with this beginning?" The group agrees.

"Do you want to go on?" Again agreement.

Leader: Let me tell you what happened next. The gang waited until
            Harry the waiter got off his shift. They wandered down to the
            river in twos and threes not to create suspicion. Each one of
            the group sneaked up on Charley's shack and looked into the
            window. It was hard to do, because the light was so bad, and
            the window so dirty. But in there they saw something that
            looked very suspicious. In groups of four, I want you to
            show me a photo tableau of what was in there as it appeared
            in the morning paper.

At this point, the players put together tableaux of the scene of the "crime."
The ideas included Charley asleep with a whiskey bottle in hand, Jimmy lying
in a pool of blood, and the cabin empty, but a note thumb-tacked to Charley's
old green table saying, "Tyrone and Dewaine. I'm okay. Don't look for me.
Jimmy."

The group chose to continue the story building on the last tableau.

Leader: Well, we know he's okay. Or he was okay when he wrote the
            note. What do we do next?

A general discussion followed. Finally one of the players suggested that
they could look around for Jimmy — maybe find Old Charley.

Leader: I have an idea. If Old Charley is down at his fishing hole, we
            might get some information out of him. Just snoop around.
            Does he know any of you guys?

Student 1: No.

Tyrone: Just Jimmy.

Student 2: Yah.

Leader: Okay, Let's get some fishing gear and find out.

            Out of role I asked who wanted to be Old Charley. One of
            the quiet boys who had added nothing to the story so far, vol-
            unteered. The original story teller said he would be Jimmy.

Waiter: All right. We've got to be cool. Nobody talk. Make like we
            are fishing, but boy what we're down there for is to . . . listen!

In the scene that followed, the players arranged themselves in a semi-circle
around the teacher's desk and blackboard. Old Charley had his bait can and
his pole. The fish weren't biting. After two minutes of serious fishing/spy-
ing, the group started to gravitate toward Old Charley and a small figure hud-
dled next to him. Charley spoke so softly, most in the room couldn't hear him.
The crowd pressed closer.

Charley: (*With emotion*) I see you, boy—sitting there. Run away from you Mama. What you think you going to do with your life?

Look at me. I was smart! I was there. My teachers all tole me I could make it. But I got mad at my mama. We had a bigfight. I even had a scholarship to college! (Pause) What did I do? I got mad and I went fishing. And look at me now. Just me and smelly old shack. No wife, no job, no friends.

Just punks like you. I coulda been somebody. I coulda been mayor. I'm smart as him. My teacher tole me I was. But you, got mad at your mama so you run away. Well, I let you stay with me for two nights, but now you gotta go home, boy. You gotta be somebody 'cause I wasn't somebody. Now go home to your mama and finish school and don't be like me!

There was a quiet moment as the whole group was visibly moved.

Leader: (*Softly*) The world really needs its Charleys, doesn't it? Charley is as much a hero as anyone you can name.

The drama lesson ended as the final bell of the day rang. The class continued to work on the story of Charley and presented a 10 minute scene of their work at Detroit's Attic Theatre's High School Showcase that spring.

LESSON PLAN FORM

LEADERS _____

PLACE _____ GRADE _____ DATE _____

1. What do you expect to achieve with your lesson?
    a. Content/Thought
    b. Group interaction
    c. Drama Goals, Objectives and Expectancies

2. What is the basis for the lesson? (Story, original idea, magazine article, etc.)

3. What are the tensions?

4. What are the built-in controls?

5. What "brotherhoods" do you expect the lesson to touch?

6. List the drama strategies and steps you plan to use to accomplish your goals.

7. What are the physical requirements?
    a. Space
    b. Props
    c. Costume pieces
    d. Writing equipment
    e. Art supplies
    f. Symbolic importance

8. Describe the roles.
    a. Leaders
    b. Players

9. List two attention arresters for the lesson

10. Make a list of 25 or more possible questions you could use in the lesson. Put some in every category.
    a. Questions that seek information
    b. Questions that give information
    c. Questions to provide control
    d. Questions to make decisions and deepen reflection

LESSON PLAN CHECK LIST

Here are considerations for planning a theatre lesson. Not every category must appear in each lesson, but the list may encourage you to think about each category before you make your final plan.

1. Tensions
2. Attention Arresters
3. Action
4. Control
5. Problem solving
6. Age appropriateness
7. Emotional content
8. Brotherhoods
9. Use of space
10. Seriousness
11. Fun
12. Content goal
13. Group goal
14. Drama Goal
15. Low or middle level role for leaders
16. Mantle of expert for group
17. Sequence of happenings
18. Alternative to sequence
19. Method of choosing child leaders
20. Use of props (real, imagined, symbolic?)
21. Use of costumes (real, imagined, symbolic?)
22. Use of other arts